020

MW01690587

...man

Pg. 29 Luther... 1st know God as enemy
35 Heb 10:30-31 Dreadful, fall into hands living God.

Pg. 140 "Meekness"

Pg. 163 " Sovereignty of God"

Tim 3:16
James 3:17
Jas. 2:19
Romans 1: 22-23
Rev 2:5
Ps. 50:12
Luke 18:11 Pharisee (Mt. 6: 1-18)... Sin Jesus hated.

Praise for R. T. Kendall:

"R. T. Kendall has given us yet another masterpiece in *Out of Your Comfort Zone*. At a time when so many in the church are trying to 'market Jesus' or 'give God a good image,' R. T. reminds us afresh that God is supreme and He is to whom we must bow. His image doesn't need modification nor spin for social relevance. Read this book and you will be encouraged."

—Michael Youssef, PhD, author of *The Power of One*

"R. T. Kendall's book exposes the heart of a shepherd concerned about the spiritual nutrition of the sheep. His refocus on the sovereignty of God is needed desperately in a day when man's dignity is sought at the expense of God's majesty. He refuses to kill the ox just to keep the stall clean as he embraces the work of the Spirit while noting the human tendency to exploit. His insistence that the God portrayed by too many is not nice should not distress us. We are not looking for nice, but purpose, and the God of purpose will constantly stretch our existing boundaries."

—Dudley Hall, president, Successful Christian Living Ministries

"Honest, courageous, hard-hitting, and discomforting."

—Lyndon Bowring

"For too many of us, God has become a 'best mate' and *nothing more*. R.T.'s passionate call to authentic relationship draws us back to the might, majesty, and holiness of 'God Most High.'"

—Eric Delve

continued . . .

"Here is the truth about God—simple, undiluted, and sadly neglected even by many evangelicals today. A must for all who want to follow Christ out of the comfort zone of respectability."

—Colin Dye

"A unique book—compelling and insightful. Engaging, easy to read, and hard to put down. A surprise in every chapter. R.T. is one of the great spiritual teachers of our time. This book will make a difference. Read it and be rewarded."

—J. John

"Very few people have R. T. Kendall's remarkable skill of making great biblical truths so accessible to the reader."

—Terry Virgo

"Here is the R.T. we know and love. Sincerely evangelical, uniquely radical, and deeply practical."

—Robert Amess

OUT OF YOUR COMFORT ZONE

Is Your God Too Nice?

R. T. KENDALL

Warner Faith

NEW YORK BOSTON NASHVILLE

Verses marked KJV are taken from the King James Version of the Bible.

First published in Great Britain in 2005 as
Out of the Comfort Zone.

Warner Faith
Hachette Book Group, USA
1271 Avenue of the Americas, New York, NY 10020

Printed in the United States of America

ISBN: 978-0-7394-7181-4

To Jack and Charles

Contents

Foreword to the American Edition

My favorite contemporary author is Dr. R. T. Kendall. His books have really blessed me for the last six years—I feed on them and find that they also feed on me. They challenge my character, my revelation of Jesus and Who He really is in my life and in my heart.

Recently I read his book, *Out of Your Comfort Zone*. I would have to honestly say I was not comfortable with this book. I do not agree totally with R. T. However, I really believe that within the Body of Christ, it is good for us to have disagreements.

I recommend the book because I believe that "iron sharpens iron." I believe you do not have to agree with every born-again believer within the Body of Christ. Should we disregard all forty of Dr. Kendall's anointed books simply because we do not agree with one? Certainly not.

I have also learned, through the years, it is good to be challenged—I have felt it was good for me and a great balance to faith teaching. It is spiritually healthy for us to examine our doctrines and our own personal walk with God.

Marilyn Hickey
Internationally known Bible teacher
Founder/President–Marilyn Hickey Ministries
November 2005

Foreword to the British Edition

There are two primary methods the devil deploys to harm or destroy the Church of Christ—*Murder* and *Mixture*. In the first he seeks to intimidate and kill God's servants, and by the second, seduce them into error. The first leads to sudden and violent death. The other draws us slowly to an inexorable death "by a thousand cuts." Of the two, the latter is surely the most dangerous, because though the first method may cause us to lose our *lives*, the second results in the complete loss of our *testimony*. The Church thus becomes a spent force, lost for words, and completely assimilated by that very world she is meant to challenge and transform by her message. The salt has not only lost its savor, but the pepper has lost its pep!

This book therefore needed to be written. Prophets are people who hear what others cannot hear, see what others cannot see, and then dare to say what others dare not say. A sense of compulsion in the heart of the author combined with the pressing needs of the hour are two of the best reasons for writing a book, and the result here is a prophetic and very timely word.

When I was a young theological student in London during the late 1970s, for two years my wife and I regularly heard Dr. R. T. Kendall preach from the historic pulpit of Westminster Chapel. I was frequently struck back then by the consistent freshness, forcefulness, and originality of his thinking, speaking, and writing. R. T. said things no one else dared to say, and said them with boldness, timeliness, and great effect. He helped impart more of both the fear of God and the comfort of God to me. I am thrilled that he continues this vital ministry to this day.

Here, R. T. tackles some of the most destructive issues seducing even Christian leaders into compromise today. The *new* isn't always the *true*, and R. T. addresses the ferment thrown up by such matters as our lame and sub-biblical concepts of God and his sovereignty and the subsequent widespread loss of the fear of God in the Church and in the world, along with our often mixed motives for ministry. He confronts our unwillingness to cause even *necessary* offense, or to take the slightest personal risk. He calls us to abandon our pseudo-religious resistance to the work of the Holy Spirit, our lack of clarity over God's judgment and hell, and our chronic reluctance to conduct our whole lives for an audience of One. Most of us really need to hear these challenges again and again.

R. T. invites us, along with the author of the Epistle to the Hebrews, to shamelessly join Jesus our Master and "*go to him outside the camp, bearing the disgrace he bore*" (Heb. 13:13). Sometimes, loyalty to Christ and his message involves the experience of being stigmatized, mocked and charged with accusations of becoming "dated" and "irrelevant" by our critics. But the best help we can offer to our wayward culture is not one of sycophantic conformity to it in both intellectual thinking and adulterated lifestyle, but to be out of step with those times, "marching to the beat of a different drum."

Unlike Samson, we dare not finish our days shorn of our power. We most accurately represent the Living God when we are truly biblical and authentically ourselves. We are most relevant when we are seemingly irrelevant. We are most likely to touch the hearts of the unfaithful when we ourselves are faithful. It is not, therefore, a case of "out with the old and in with the new," but rather, "out with the old and *in with the even older*"! We are to make it our aim to *get back to the Bible.*

This book is for all those who want to know how to "rock the boat" for Jesus. R. T. attempts to show us here precisely how we can do this. In my view, he has succeeded admirably.

Greg Haslam
Minister, Westminster Chapel, London
July 2004

Preface to the American Edition

I am in my comfort zone when pursuing my hobby called bone-fishing—a sport that is only done in the Florida Keys where we now live. The bonefish are called that because they are very bony—you don't eat them. It is strictly a sport that combines hunting and fishing. If you catch one, you throw him back into the water to live. To catch bonefish you must quietly and carefully stalk them, looking for them with great patience and casting only when you see them. The bonefish is a wily and very skittish fish. He is hard to see, hard to catch. But if you hook a bonefish he takes off like a torpedo. There is nothing quite like it. You can go days without even seeing one. However, the expectancy of seeing and getting one to take your bait is so exciting that you are willing to look for them all day, for catching a bonefish is a thrill you never get over. It is the quintessence of my comfort zone!

When my new publisher Time Warner showed me their suggestion for the cover of this book, I was immediately reminded of something that happened to me. I was fishing on a bonefish flat near Key Largo, finding dozens of bonefish all around me. One can wait months to see this many at one time. I had not seen so many in years. I lost all concept of time. I was busy casting to them when suddenly my boat wouldn't move. It was stuck on the bottom. I was horrified. I couldn't believe this would happen to me. The tide had run out so swiftly that I had not noticed. I got out of the boat and tried pushing the boat into deeper water. The boat still wouldn't move. All I could do was to wait for several hours for the tide to come in. I was utterly out of my comfort zone!

The book you hold in your hand was first published in the United Kingdom, out-selling (so far) all my other books. I am not sure why, but it obviously struck a chord with many British Christians. Jonathan Edwards taught that the task of every generation is to discover in which direction the Sovereign Redeemer is moving, then move in that direction. To find where God is at work today—not yesterday—often requires that we go outside our comfort zone.

This is my first book with Time Warner. I want to thank Rolf Zettersten for his willingness to publish this book. Perhaps this is because he too is a bonefisherman! Working with my new editor Gary Terashita has been a delight.

I thank Marilyn Hickey for writing the Foreword to the U.S. edition. I salute her for her courage in commending a book which is out of her own comfort zone in certain places.

It is my fervent prayer that this book will be a surprising blessing to you and bring great honor and glory to God.

R. T. Kendall
November 2005
Key Largo, Florida
www.rtkendallministries.com

Preface to the British Edition

This is the most difficult book I have written, from several standpoints. First, I wrote this book chapter after chapter with fear and trembling, knowing it might not make me many friends and also causing me to worry if I might even lose some! I did not intend it to be controversial but I fear, upon reflection, it may be seen that way. I have never liked being controversial, much less to be seen in that manner, but sometimes I suppose you cannot help it.

Second, I have struggled to get this book done. Never before have I had so much trouble with computers, for example. On more than one occasion I lost whole chapters by pushing the wrong button on my computer. After the book was completely written, with a rereading and final editing still to be done, we had a storm here in the Florida Keys and the electricity went off. When it came back on my work of several days of editing and correcting was down the drain. I don't know how it happened but it did.

Third, we wrestled over what to call this book. My original title was "Your God Is Too Nice," borrowing of course from J. B. Phillips' classic *Your God Is Too Small.* But friends I trust persuaded me against it. And then, once it was completed, one of them decided that was the best title after all! But by then Hodder already had the cover designed and finished. I think my friends feared I would put the reader off by a title that was too forbidding—or that I would make people think I was presenting a God who was overly harsh and remote. Rob Parsons, for one, said, "R. T., nobody has persuaded me more than you that God is for me—are you going to write a book that takes this away?" No! Thus I was all the more careful to preserve our teaching on the mercy and tenderness of God.

I once promised Rob Parsons I would never again ask him to read a manuscript, knowing how busy he is. He has helped me so much with previous books, among them *The Anointing, In Pursuit of His Glory,* and *Thanking God,* for a start. But I went to him on bended knee again, because I needed a sharp mind who would tell me not what I wanted to hear but what I needed to hear. People like Roband Lyndon Bowring are among those whose wisdom I am so blessed to have the benefit of. But there are others: Robert Amess and Colin Dye in the UK, and Dr. Harry Kilbride, Robert Ferguson, and Richard Oates in the USA. And of course Beryl Grogan, my former secretary, for her invaluable role in helping us put the book together. This is to say nothing about my wife, Louise, who is always faithful in telling me what I need to change—or leave out. Our friend Nancy Wall did a good bit of research for me in the preparation of this book. I thank God for every bit of wisdom and loving criticism I received from these.

It was my editor David Moloney of Hodder & Stoughton who came up with the title of this book: *Out of the Comfort Zone:*

Is Your God Too Nice? I do feel at the end of the day this one works best and says pretty much what I want to convey. As always, it is a pleasure to work with David and his staff at Hodder. I thank Trisha Dale who has done the copyediting and also Julie Hatherall for her input. I am grateful to God that He has given me favor with Charles Nettleton and the people of Hodder.

I am especially grateful that my brilliant successor Greg Haslam, minister of Westminster Chapel, has written the wonderful Foreword. He too has made suggestions which I have taken on board. I knew he would agree with the thrust of this book and I am so happy for the ongoing relationship with him and my former friends and members of the Chapel.

Finally, this book is dedicated to my two close friends and colleagues Jack Taylor and Charles Carrin. When Louise and I came to America in February 2002 I was virtually unknown and without any ministry in the United States. They have opened doors for me through the three of us holding Word, Spirit and Power conferences all over America. I love these men very much and with honor and deep affection I dedicate this volume to them.

R. T. Kendall
Key Largo, Florida
www.rtkendallministries.com
September 2004

Out of Your Comfort Zone

Introduction
The Man Who Was Known in Hell

> Jesus I know, and I know about Paul, but who are you?
>
> ACTS 19:15

Nearly fifty years ago, when Paul Cain was the young boy wonder known as a faith healer and prophet, he held nightly services in a church in the Midwest. One night as he was preaching a lady stood and began speaking in tongues while he spoke. He stopped preaching and asked her please to stop what she was doing as it was disruptive, certainly not in the Spirit, and utterly out of order. The following night as he preached she again began speaking in tongues. He stopped and asked again that she refrain but warned her this time that he would reveal what the Lord had shown him about her if she did not stop. On the third night she repeated the same behavior. Once again Paul warned her to stop, again stating that he would reveal what the Lord had shown him about her. She continued.

He then looked at her squarely and announced that not only was she not in the Spirit, but that she was living in immorality. And there was more: The man with whom she was having an affair was seated right there in the congregation. Paul pointed him out before all present and stated that this man was planning to leave his own wife and children for her after this very service was over.

The woman stopped. All was deathly quiet.

But that isn't the end of the story. After the service, just before the host pastor of the church took Paul to his hotel, the pastor said, "Paul, I am closing down the meeting."

"Why?" said Paul. "The services are going okay."

"Well," said the pastor, "nobody is being converted and I feel we should discontinue having services."

"Oh," said Paul to the pastor. "That is not the reason you are stopping the meeting. You are closing down the meeting because I revealed what was going on between the lady and that man seated not far from her—because that very man has promised to give you a million dollars for your new church building."

"That's a lie," the pastor countered abruptly.

"Oh, I wish you had not said that," said Paul tearfully. "You will not live to preach in your new building."

"Now Paul, don't say that. Please take that back."

"I'm so sorry," Paul replied. "I cannot take it back."

The pastor pleaded, "Please, Paul, don't say that. Look, when things settle down, I will have you back to preach."

Two years later and several hundred miles away from that city, Paul received a phone call from a member of that same church in the Midwest. It was the day of the dedication of the new church building. The pastor had suffered a heart attack in the lobby as he was walking into the auditorium and had been taken to a hospital. Would Paul please pray for the pastor? But the pastor died two weeks later without returning to the church.

There is something worse, however, than the story I just related. I have to report that since I wrote the above lines—in other words, after this book you hold in your hands was originally finished and edited—it is now in the public domain that this same Paul Cain is a fallen hero. He has been involved in a moral failure and will no longer be in the ministry. He is now yesterday's man, like King Saul, as I wrote in my book *The Anointing: Yesterday, Today, Tomorrow*. I never dreamed in my wildest imagination this could happen to him. But God has judged this venerable prophet in an unmistakable manner. It puts in bolder relief than anything I could say in this book that God is no respecter of persons and will bend the rules for none of us. I can only think of King Saul who had such a brilliant beginning (see 1 Sam. 10:9, 11:7) and who continued to prophesy even while trying to kill David (1 Sam. 19:23f). How does one explain his gift being in operation even though the Lord had departed from him (1 Sam. 18:12)? It is because the gifts and calling of God are irrevocable (Rom. 11:29).

As I write these lines Paul Cain, aged seventy-five, is somewhere in seclusion. Those who have been blessed by his ministry will be shocked. He was the last person I would have anticipated to become yesterday's man. I thought I knew him fairly well. But I have also said many times that those people I began to admire too much disappointed me sooner or later. It is equally a reminder that God will deal with you and me if we are not accountable to trusted and reliable people. Peter said that judgment must begin at the house of God (1 Pet. 4:17)—and that is certainly what has happened in the case of Paul Cain. I do not see any way he can be used again. He will now possibly be remembered more for his failure than his stunning prophecies. A nice God overlooks sin. But the God of the Bible is not nice.

Whatever is so wrong with being nice? I certainly want to be nice. But, given the way that word can be used today, I am not sure I always want to be known as nice. I have done a little research on the word, even tracing its history from the fifteenth century. Then it bore little resemblance to the way it is understood today. That is no doubt why you do not find the word "nice" once in the King James Version of the Bible (also known as the Authorized Version of 1611). "Nice" is more of a modern, essentially tepid word, like water that is neither cold nor hot but merely lukewarm. Using "nice" as a descriptor today is sometimes (though not always) a cunning way to "damn with faint praise" when we don't particularly admire or like a person. "He's a nice man," you might say.

Today, the word "nice" is generally used two ways—meaning either "likable" or that someone or something is "precise." It is the first category we have in mind in this book or, to extract from various dictionaries: to be inoffensive, people-pleasing, safe, cooperative, sweet, harmless, well-mannered, friendly, hunky-dory, groovy, lovely, seemly, winsome, agreeable, delightful, ducky, or yielding (Merriam-Webster).

Someone helping me with my research on this book labeled a folder "Nice God." It made me laugh. It's the way I might approach a dog if I am unsure if he is friendly, saying "Nice dog, nice puppy, nice dog." And yet I think many want to feel exactly that way about God, saying "Nice God, nice God."

This book is not intended to be critical of any particular person. Though certain people or movements enter my mind when I am discussing a particular situation that I feel needs to be addressed, my desire is not to make another feel they should take something personally. To be totally candid, I need the truth to which this book points more than anybody. I know what it is to be convicted when I preach and in fact I have been convicted as I wrote this book. What follows therefore hits me right, left and center.

And yet I wrote *Worshipping God* when I still had so much to learn about worship; *Total Forgiveness* when I was still struggling; *Pure Joy* when I knew I needed joy more than anybody I knew. So do not think I am on a pedestal looking down at you or anyone else. The truth is, I have learned over the years that often as I am preaching or writing I am on a steep learning curve myself.

I had the privilege of having Dr. George Buttrick as a visiting professor of preaching when I was at Southern Baptist Theological Seminary years ago. He was an old-fashioned liberal and I got little out of his writings or even his preaching, but I will never forget one thing he hammered into us, although I fear I still have plenty left to learn on this point: "Never moralize." To Dr. Buttrick, preaching that is constantly moralizing, telling off the audience, or pointing a finger is not good preaching. I think he was almost right, though not entirely, however, because the Word of God was given to us partly for rebuking (2 Tim. 3:16). Yet I knew what he meant. I pray with all my heart that what you read will not make you feel "told off." Even if these words hit where it hurts. I pray you feel the Holy Spirit lovingly seeking to get your attention, just as God has been so gentle with me when getting my attention. I can never forget James 3:17: "But the wisdom that is from above is first pure, then peaceable, gentle, and easy to be intreated, full of mercy and good fruits, without partiality, and without hypocrisy" (KJV). O Lord, let this book be full of mercy!

I want this book to bring us back to the God of the Bible. Not the God you like or the way you wish He were. We must seek the very God of the Bible—unembellished and unvarnished—as He really is. This does not mean you will like Him. I am not going to make Him likable, because by our very small, human standards, He simply isn't always a nice God. For some this book might even be an introduction to the God of the Bible. I wonder how many people know Him, or even know much about Him. Do you? After all, this is the only God there is. There is no other save the true God who is portrayed, unveiled, and presented in the Bible from Genesis to Revelation.

I was trained at Southern Baptist Theological Seminary before it became the theologically conservative institution it is today. When I was there over thirty years ago there were teachers and professors who would unashamedly say, "I know Paul said that in Romans, but I disagree with Paul. I know Luke said that, but I disagree with him."

Within the Christian Church today, speaking generally, there are those who admittedly and openly dislike the God of the Bible. They say so. They refer to the Bible only when a verse or point of view in Holy Scripture happens to cohere with their own. But there are also those who claim to adhere to and love the God of the Bible but interpret Him in such a manner that He becomes . . . nice. Just nice. The Church today, speaking generally, has lost its way.

I fear that the God many people worship today is Feuerbach's God. Ludwig Feuerbach (1804–1872), the German philosopher whose writings laid the foundation for the philosophy of Karl Marx, claimed that God is nothing more than man's projection upon the backdrop of the universe. His point was this: Ordinary people need and want very much to believe there is a God or someone "up there" who is looking after them and who will give them heaven when they die. This is a creation of the mind prompted by a need for a God to help when problems arise—God is their crutch. This God exists in our imagination and, though this is subjective, we nonetheless objectify Him, as it were, and put Him "there" so we can believe in Him and worship Him. This is basically what Feuerbach taught on this matter.

He had a point. Sadly, many of us in the modern Church have done just what he suggested. We are embarrassed about the God of the Bible, especially the God of the Old Testament, and even the teachings of Jesus and the apostles when it comes to both the need and the only way to be saved, God's right to judge and, last but not least, hell. So we attempt to have our cake and eat it too; we claim to believe the Bible but water down so much of what it clearly says that we become quite comfortable with "our God," thank you very much, who is simply—for want of a better descriptive adjective—nice. Lovely. Sweet. Groovy. Cool. Neat.

But is that the total picture? I don't think so. I want to say some things in this book I believe need to be said. I have waited for someone else to do it. In my research I have come across an article or two, "Your God Is too Nice" or "Your God Is too Safe," but as far as I know there is no book addressing some of the topics I feel compelled to bring up in this book. I want to call a spade a spade and our God what He truly is based on the composite picture the Bible offers up. The truth is, we all need help in this area. Perhaps some people want God to only look nice. Others are embarrassed that a number of our forebears, some educated, some uneducated, stressed things about God that do not appeal to non-Christians today. Such forbears gave Christianity, it is believed, a bad name. We have inherited this, and we want to shed this image once and for all. Some theology departments and seminaries have consequently sought to turn out ministers and clergymen who will give God better press. Some Christians are also sensitive to the criticism that non-Christians may have for the Church; they want to be accepted so say, "Hang on, that isn't what I believe," as if this will cause everybody to say, "Oh, good! Now I want to be a Christian." Yet has our apologizing for the way God is perceived by many worked? Has it brought tens of thousands into our churches?

No. You know it and I know it.

I would like to think that if we stopped apologizing for God, or gave up trying to make Him look appealing, we would have greater success. Yet maybe not. But I know we would have His approval. If we will thoughtfully hold up the God of the Bible as He Himself chose to describe Himself in His Word, I believe He will honor this. I would predict that to the degree we do, the Holy Spirit will work to convert more and more people and bring greater awareness of the true God than to any extent previously seen.

When I refer to the term "apology," the reader should know this word is used generally two ways. One usage is "to make an excuse for"—that is, to apologize and say one is sorry for a spoken word or other action. I fear this is the kind of apology that has prevailed in many places. There is another use of the word which is valid—that is "to make intellectual claims for the God of the Bible that can be defended and tested by reason and facts." This latter type of apology is sometimes needed, as long as it is the one true God being defended.

Yet the "Nice God" I am uneasy with is the one people are increasingly beginning to perceive and portray in many quarters, and He is not big enough, strong enough, awesome enough, or knowledgeable enough to harm a flea.

One of my predecessors at Westminster Chapel, Dr. Martyn Lloyd-Jones, often used to make me laugh when he would say, "The trouble with the Church today is that it has too many nice men in the ministry." I think he felt the Church needed men who were not always so pleasant but rather more rugged and unafraid to step on people's toes. Is he right? Do you think many in the ministry are nice? Look around. Would you say most of the ministers, pastors, church leaders, and clergymen whom you know are nice people? If so, was Dr. Lloyd-Jones right that this is not a good thing?

Would people who know me call me a nice man? (I suspect many would.) And yet it does not matter what people call you or me. I once heard Paul Cain say, "I am too old now to disobey God." I know exactly what he meant. He did not mean he could *not* disobey God, for we never outgrow the potential for disobedience. Instead Paul was saying he has a limited number of days and years left to live, and he cannot afford to fall short of what honors the true God. The same goes for me. I do not want to waste the time I have left being a pleaser of people, catering to the majority, avoiding the truth, or living as a fraud.

As I said in my book *The Anointing: Yesterday, Today, Tomorrow*, there are by nature two things we all want to avoid: moving outside our comfort zone, and stigma. Our Nice God keeps us safe and snug in our comfort zone. So many of us have satisfied ourselves with a belief in God—that is enough. I think of James' admonition: "You believe that there is one God. Good! Even the demons believe that—and shudder" (Jas. 2:19). But do we shudder? Are we afraid of our God? Probably not. Yet we should be. Once we project Nice God on the backdrop of the universe we comfort ourselves in one stroke and think our duty is done. Nothing else bothers us; we're in good shape. We don't need a thing. And yet in that moment the One whose eyes are like a flame of fire says on His throne: "You do not realize that you are wretched, pitiful, poor, blind and naked" (Rev. 3:17). Friends, our tepid, lukewarm devotion to the God of the Bible makes Him sick and He is ready to spit us out of His mouth.

One of my fears in publishing this book is that it will play to the gallery of self-righteous Christians who will agree with the message in this book and say, "Good! Give it to them." I hope not, as it will not bless me nor probably honor God if they do. Instead, I hope this book will make a definite difference in people. Good people. Nice people. Not-so-nice people. Because I want to stir you up, not play into any part of your comfort zone. Nice isn't good enough.

We need a fearless, rugged commitment to the God of the Bible for which we are prepared to die. My friend Joseph Tson says, "The most dangerous person in the world is a person who is not afraid to die." We need Christians who are a threat to Satan as much as certain terrorists are to the West. I wish I were that. We are too much like the sons of Sceva who were intrigued with the supernatural underworld but no threat to Satan. Indeed, the devil didn't even know them! When trying to cast out devils in Jesus' name, claiming to know Paul and promoting themselves to the level of their incompetence, they were utterly overcome by demonic powers (Acts 19:16). They *tried* using Jesus' name but the evil spirit answered, "Jesus I know, and I know about Paul, but who are you?" (Acts 19:15).

My old friend Rolfe Barnard used to preach a sermon entitled "The Man Who Was Known in Hell" (based on the aforementioned verse). In other words, Paul was a real threat to Satan; he was well known by the devil. "I want to be known in hell," said Rolfe in that unforgettable sermon. But are we? I don't mean to be unfair, but do you really think you are a threat to the devil? A commitment to Christ inspires action that Satan can't help but notice. Is Satan aware of you? Is he working overtime to keep you and your eternal love of Christ from threatening his interests?

- How much do you talk to the lost at a personal level and try to win them to Jesus Christ?
- How far are you prepared to go in your commitment to Him?
- How willing are you to be led outside your comfort zone—or do you privately resent that this could be asked of you?
- Are you rid of all bitterness and grudges, and do you *totally* forgive those who have hurt you? (Satan cannot work through a person who is free of bitterness, and God won't widely use the person who is vindictive.)
- Do you willingly accept every trial God allows, or do you complain and grumble the whole time?
- How much, how regularly, and how sacrificially, do you give financially to the Lord? And, oh yes, how much do you actually pray every day?

Satan trembles when he sees
The weakest saint upon his knees.

WILLIAM COWPER (1731–1800)

I sometimes fear that I am not a threat to Satan. Do I want to be? Yes. Think of those people who are a threat to the whole world! I want to be a threat to all that is evil. Our reward administered at the judgment seat of Christ will not be based on whether we were liked or admired by other Christians, or even whether we built up a good reputation among the saints. We won't be recognized because we are famous. Instead, I wonder if our reward will be given on the basis of whether we were known in hell and served as a constant threat to Satan and his fallen angels.

Those who accomplish great things for God on this planet will be known in hell because they have a reputation in the underworld for being a threat to all of Satan's interests. I would predict that the man or woman who accomplishes the greatest things for God and His kingdom will be unashamed of the Bible generally and the gospel particularly, devoid of bitterness, totally forgiving, full of the love of Christ, sexually pure, fearless in standing for righteousness, unafraid to die for what they believe, self-disciplined, valuing the opinion of God more than people's applause, enjoying intimacy with the Holy Spirit, impervious to the love of money and material things, unable to be bought off or bribed, faithful in prayer, sacrificial and regular in the giving of their finances, gentle, continually prepared to move outside their comfort zone and, last but not least, *known in hell.*

But our comfort zones let us feel at ease day and night, no matter what we do or where we go. We bring God into everything, supposing He is thrilled. I witnessed one female Hollywood performer come on stage wearing the most sensual, provocative dress (truly, she was wearing almost nothing), and say that she prays to God before she faces the audience, claiming He helps her perform! In America we have grown accustomed to heavyweight boxers interviewed after the fight saying, "Thank you, Lord, for letting me win." I was once asked to pray for a professional football team in Miami before they went on the field. I did. I knew the other team had a minister praying for them as well. I could have refused, but I took advantage of the ten minutes to preach that they also gave me, and then I prayed everyone would have the right attitude, no matter who won. I don't know if I did good or harm, but I do know I was edging awfully close to Nice God.

Stigma isn't nice. Defined for our purposes as "a mark of shame or discredit" (Merriam-Webster), bearing a stigma or causing offense isn't fun. The most truthful thing I think I can say about today's gospel, speaking generally, is that it is de-stigmatized. So often it seems there is a concerted effort when the name of Jesus is uttered to de-stigmatize the gospel.

It is my wish and sincere prayer that this book will drive us to our knees and move us to seek the face of the God of the Bible. We must get to know Him and love Him for being exactly as He is. We must stop wanting to change Him and be unashamed of Him wherever we go. Peter said that judgment must begin with the family of God (1 Pet. 4:17). If we cannot criticize ourselves we are very insecure indeed. But I suspect the judgment that is needed is far more than self-criticism, but rather to come face to face with God's own feelings regarding the Church that bears His name. He is not happy with it.

·1·

When God Plays Hard to Get

> If I were hungry I would not tell you . . .
>
> PSALM 50:12

It seems to me that the modern Church has drifted so far from the biblical revelation of the true God that any resemblance between Him and the popular God of today's generation is quite remote. I think we are in a Romans 1 situation:

> Although they claimed to be wise, they became fools and exchanged the glory of the immortal God for images made to look like mortal man and birds and animals and reptiles. (Rom. 1:22–23)

It is a case in which the God of the Bible is either too holy or too terrible for us, so we have come up with a God we are at home with. We can thus feel sufficiently religious without having to identify with the ancient God of Israel and the earliest Church.

During seminary I was required to read a book about God

in which the author managed to concoct a God whereby one need not be regarded as an atheist after all, even though the God of the Bible was rejected. Theologian Paul Tillich (1886–1965) even suggested that an atheist might be a believer when faith was defined as "ultimate concern."

This book is not an attack on liberalism in the modern Church. I fear that those who deny the historic truths of Holy Scripture are beyond the pale and most likely very hard to reach. Rather, those closer to home worry me, those who seem to want to hold on to the Bible up to a point yet distance themselves from disturbing realities we all know are contained in Holy Scripture.

As Ludwig Feuerbach opined, people want to believe in something, especially a God who will take care of them in times of trouble and then give them a home in heaven when they die, and so they mentally project such a God and claim He really does exist. Of course such a God does not exist, says Feuerbach, outside of their minds where He brings comfort.

It is my view that many Christians do this. They know full well there are things in the Bible they don't want to believe, but they are not prepared to throw out everything in the Bible so they fancy a God who approves of their own comfort zone. This God is happy with Christians who reject Bible-denying liberal theology while at the same time approving of their unease with the total revelation of God as revealed in the Old and New Testament. In fact, some of these people will go so far as to claim they believe in the whole of the Bible—from Genesis to maps while ensuring they are at ease in their folk religion. They have been baptized and, in some cases, confirmed; they are almost certainly approved of by their church leader; they attend church to varying degrees of regularity and feel quite right in themselves.

What does God think of this? Is He so neglected by the masses that He is simply thrilled to have anybody anywhere, whatever their level of conviction, give Him any attention at all? Is God so starved for recognition that He will make any measure of concession to any person who makes an effort, however small, to acknowledge Him? Will God therefore show His approval toward any kind of profession of faith because some tipping of the hat toward Him is better than nothing?

The nice God of today's religious people might do just that, but not the God of the Bible. Unless He chooses to withhold His real feelings and intentions from us for awhile, which is the basis of this chapter.

One reason I abandoned "Your God Is Too Nice" as a title is because I didn't want to make the reader feel guilty or think I feel qualified to judge you. I write out of my experience of over fifty years of preaching, most of which have been as a pastor.

If God is too nice, what does this mean? Perhaps you have been worshipping a God you can be comfortable with but who is not the God of the Bible at all. And yet it could mean that the true God has decided to be nice to you for the moment and let you remain in your comfort zone, undisturbed. "But this isn't being very nice at all if He will eventually show that He is unhappy with me," you say. True, but what if He tried for a while but you wouldn't listen? He then let you carry on as if nothing happened. What if He simply decided to be "nice" to you by letting you remain in your comfort zone and instead seeking a person elsewhere who will listen to Him?

Rodney Howard-Browne told me that the Lord put it to him like this, "If you don't do what I tell you I will find someone who will." Jesus said to the church at Ephesus, "If you do not repent, I will come to you and remove your lampstand from its place" (Rev. 2:5). This is what happens when a church goes astray or soft and God raises up movements to carry on with what ought to have been the Church's own mandate.

Arthur Blessitt, the man who has carried a cross around the world, said that as a university student he prayed in his dormitory room, "God, give me a work nobody else will do."

A woman once asked Arthur, "Why does God speak to you but not to me?"

"Have you ever felt an impulse to speak to someone about Jesus that you didn't know?" he asked.

"As a matter of fact, I have," she said.

Arthur then said to her, "Start obeying that voice and it will become clearer and clearer."

One of the most stunning lines I have come across is in Psalm 50:12: "If I were hungry I would not tell you, for the world is mine, and all that is in it." That evening our children were sitting on the floor in front of me watching television, and not being too interested in what they were watching, I found myself reading that verse. I began to feel very uneasy. *I wish the Lord would tell me if he were hungry.* Then my thoughts traveled to wondering if God wanted me to spend more time with Him than I had been giving Him. If so, would He tell me? The phrase "If I were hungry I would not tell you" troubled me. I couldn't shake it off. I read it again. And again. I began to get the definite feeling that God was telling me He needed and wanted me after all.

The context of this verse in Psalm 50 is that, though the world is His and although He has cattle on a thousand hills, my God is hungry for me. Though He has countless angels beyond millions and billions, not to mention other people all over the world worshipping Him and spending time with Him, He wanted me. I seized the moment, for some reason. I decided to fast the next day. I sought His face as I had not done before. Yet the curious thing was, God was hinting the very opposite of what He was saying in Psalm 50:12.

The unveiling of that verse was part of a process that led me to one of the most unusual teachings I have ever come across in Scripture. I have racked my brain many times over what to call this teaching and I still struggle with the best term or phrase for it. I used to call it "the divine tease" in our School of Theology at Westminster Chapel. By that term I meant God's somewhat playful but deadly serious setup to let us find out what is in our hearts. Essentially, it is when He says or does the very opposite of what He intends for us to perceive. But I have since decided to refer to this startling and profound truth as *when God plays hard to get.* For He does! You might think this isn't fair. Perhaps not. I still struggle with Jeremiah's words, "O LORD, you deceived me, and I was deceived" (Jer. 20:7). I don't claim to know all that this means. The theme of this chapter is therefore but the tip of the iceberg of a most extraordinary teaching.

Perhaps the best introduction to this truth is when Jesus was walking to Emmaus with two people who were kept from recognizing who He really was. It was the same day He had been raised from the dead. They came to this village and, when it was time to say good-bye, Jesus "acted as if he were going further."

This was not His intention at all. He fully intended to stay with them a while longer. He had more to show them. But He did not tell them so and they certainly did not know. Jesus "acted" as if He were going farther, and He played the role so well the two men were clearly going to be upset if He did leave them. The truth is, Jesus wanted them to do exactly as they did—to plead with Him to stay with them. They didn't know they were persuading Jesus to do precisely what He planned for them: "They urged him strongly, 'Stay with us, for it is nearly evening; the day is almost over.' So he [Jesus] went in to stay with them" (Luke 24:29).

When God plays hard to get, then, He often means the very opposite of what He says. And yet it is only because God wants us to plead with Him when He appears not to care, whether we do or not. This particular aspect of God's unusual way of dealing with us is often in operation when our circumstances suggest it is okay this time to put first other things beside God for the day. If I am so busy, and God knows this, He surely does not expect me to spend time alone with Him praying and reading my Bible. If I am in debt and can't pay my bills, He surely does not expect me to return my tithes to Him. If there are important people who want to see me, He surely would want me to put these people ahead of ordinary souls. If I did not sleep well last night, He understands this and surely would not expect me to try to have my usual quiet time.

Listen to these words from Martin Luther's journal: "I have a very busy day today. I must spend not two hours, but three, in prayer." For most of us facing that situation, we would spend less time in prayer, but to Luther it meant he must spend more time in prayer than ever in order to receive divine help to get more done! The movers and shakers and great saints in church history recognized when God plays hard to get—even if they did not call it that.

Why does God do it? To see what is in our hearts. It is not for Him as He already knows. It is for us. It lets us see the truth about ourselves. The truth of this "side" of God, if I may put it that way, brings out the truth of what we *want;* it brings our true feelings to the surface. Although they did not have a clue at first He was Jesus, the two people on the road to Emmaus had been captivated by His teaching. When our hearts burn within us it is a wonderful, wonderful sign that God is at work and wants us to seek His face. A burning heart is there not to mock us but to prod us to seek His face.

And what do you suppose motivated them then and would do it now for us? You might say, "If Jesus were here playing hard to get, I would urge Him to stay too, just like those two men. They had Jesus interpreting Scripture for them. If He did that with me, I too would plead with Him to stay around." Quite right, but the men didn't even know it was Jesus. The truth and the application of the Scripture He taught is what set their hearts on fire.

It is a strong hint to us when the truth of the Word of God has this kind of effect. Charles Spurgeon used to say to preachers, "When a text gets a hold of you, chances are you have got a hold of it." It is because God is at work to draw us closer to Himself than ever. It is His way of subtly beckoning to us to seek His face. On that night when I kept reading the words, "If I were hungry I would not tell you," I was gripped and did not know why. It turned out that God was telling me He yearned for me to spend more time with Him. It was a demonstration of God playing hard to get. He hides His face from us, just as He did with Hezekiah: "God left him to test him and to know everything that was in his heart" (2 Chron. 32:31).

Another time Jesus was watching when the disciples were rowing against the wind and waves on the Sea of Galilee. Jesus had gone up into a mountain to pray and from His vantage point He could see the disciples struggling. I am fascinated how Jesus did not immediately go to help them. Instead, he watched them. Would it not have been nice had Jesus left His place on the mountain at once and turned up on the sea to help them? Could He not have interceded for them by asking the Father to stop the wind? But He only watched them.

Yet He does this with all of us. He sees us in our struggle and anxieties and does not step in. There these disciples were, "straining at the oars," with Jesus doing nothing to rescue them! He waited until four o'clock in the morning before He showed up. Then when He did so, walking on the water, He was "about to pass by them." So He wasn't even going to identify Himself, and they too were kept from recognizing Him; they thought He was a ghost. But Jesus chose at that moment to intervene and said, "Take courage! It is I. Don't be afraid" (Mark 6:47–51; Matt. 14:22–27). God is never too late and never too early; He's always right on time.

Consider the Syrophoenician woman of Mark 7:24–30. She was not Jewish but Greek, yet she still approached Jesus and begged Him to drive a demon out of her daughter. Jesus treated her with an almost callous coldness. " 'First let the children eat all they want,' he told her, 'for it is not right to take the children's bread and toss it to their dogs' " (v. 27). If the Lord said those words to many of us we would walk away in disgust and sarcastically say, "Thanks a lot, sorry to be such a nuisance to you,"—and never know what might have been our lot had we persisted as this woman did. Instead of being offended, acknowledging what would be an insult by today's reckoning, and going away in a huff, she reasoned with him: " 'Yes, Lord, but even the dogs under the table eat the children's crumbs' " (v. 28). She knew her place and realized Jesus owed her nothing. Jesus told her, " 'For such a reply, you may go; the demon has left your daughter' " (v. 29).

A widespread feeling exists among people today that God owes us something, that if we do something good or righteous, God should stand at attention and salute us. Our self-righteousness creeps in and we say to ourselves, "Most people don't even go to church at all. This puts me in a special class;

therefore God should be very happy that I am doing this good deed." The good deed might be attending church, tithing, or spending extra time in prayer. We think God should reward those of us whom we assume are a cut above most people.

My wife, Louise, was miraculously healed in 1995 when Rodney and Adonica Howard-Browne laid hands on her and prayed for her. They invited her to come to Lakeland, Florida, to attend a camp meeting there. She agreed to go. When she walked in the first night, nothing went right. Thousands of people were there, strange people doing what seemed to her very weird things. The people around her seat were even rude, so she got up and moved to another area. She really wanted to go back to the hotel, pack her bags, and get on the next plane back to England. But she stayed. She phoned me two days later to say of the camp meeting, "It is the nearest you get to heaven without dying; it is the greatest experience of my life" (a sentiment I promised myself I would not take too personally). Louise was never to be the same again; those days in Lakeland were more precious than gold, but she initially had every reason to reject the whole experience.

You might think God would be nice and immediately acknowledge those who sincerely seek His face with a tangible sign on a silver platter. He might have been nice to Martin Luther the night that courageous man stood before the authorities at Worms, Germany, in the sixteenth century. After all, Luther was standing alone for the gospel, the truth of God's own Word. But Luther walked back and forth in his cell that final night before the trial crying out to his Lord, "O God, are you dead?" No angelic visitation. No congratulations. No sense of God. Only silence. But the next day Luther uttered words that changed history: "Here I stand. I can do no other. God help me. Amen." God wants us to accept His ways and affirm Him *as He is* rather than seeing Him only how we may want Him to be. When we are out of our comfort zone we can learn His ways.

> "For my thoughts are not your thoughts, neither are your ways my ways," declares the LORD. "As the heavens are higher than the earth, so are my ways higher than your ways and my thoughts than your thoughts." (Isa. 55:8–9)

Moses was possibly the greatest leader of men and women in world history. He was a brilliant military strategist. He understood people and their feelings. He had an extremely high degree of patience, and he did not take rejection personally. This man knew what it was to be loved by his people as well as being hated and rejected.

Things were so bad on one occasion that God stepped in and made a deal with Moses. It was a proposition most leaders I know would have latched onto with both hands. It went something like this: God said, "Moses, these people who are supposed to be following you are a sorry lot. I am tired of them, and I know you are too. Here is what I am going to do: I will destroy them. Yes, I will wipe them off the face of the earth and start all over again with you as the leader." Though paraphrased, this is essentially what God said; read it in Exodus 32:9–10 (Num. 14:11–12). Moses wasted no time in replying to the offer:

> Then the Egyptians will hear about it! . . . They have already heard that you, O LORD, are with these people and that you, O LORD, have been seen face to face, that your cloud stays over them, and that you go before them in a pillar of cloud by day and a pillar of fire by night. If you put these people to

> death all at one time, the nations who have heard this report about you will say, "The LORD was not able to bring these people into the land he promised them on oath; so he slaughtered them in the desert." (Num. 14:13–16)

Moses then reminded the Lord that He was "slow to anger and abounding in love" and interceded for the people to be forgiven (v. 18). Had Moses not been knowledgeable in God's ways—or cared more about his own ego—he would have said "Yes, kill these unworthy people, Lord." The psalmist picked up on this event and said, "So he said he would destroy them—had not Moses, his chosen one, stood in the breach before him to keep his wrath from destroying them" (Ps. 106:23).

It was God playing hard to get. God wanted Moses to respond exactly as he did. Had he taken the Lord's words seriously when God said, "Let's start all over again and I will make a new nation," Moses would have shown he did not know the Lord very well. Moses had developed such a love for the glory of God that his personal feelings and ego were subservient to the honor. Moses did not value his own reputation and esteem as much as he cared about how the world thought about the Lord. Through this experience God also let Moses see for himself that he was getting to know the Lord's very ways, which was the key to his greatness. There are not many leaders like Moses.

God also played hard to get in the case of King Saul (see 1 Sam. 13:1–15). But Saul failed to see it and lost the privilege of passing on the kingship to his family. What happened? The prophet Samuel had agreed to be present at a critical time but was overdue for some reason and kept Saul waiting. Nobody knew what was really going on. It was a divine setup to see what Saul would do. Would the new king honor the word of God?

Would he stick to the ways of God as revealed in Scripture or would he presume he represented an exception to the revelation of God? Had Saul done what was right he would have said, "Let's not be hasty. We will wait for Samuel before there is any administering of the burnt offerings because he is the only one the Lord would approve of for this." If only.

How many of us have done this? In church and during a time of inspiration we may sing "Have Thine Own Way, Lord" or some devotional hymn by which we pledge to get closer to Him. We tell Him we want more anointing, that we want to please Him in all our ways. Others will go forward at the end of a service and promise the Lord all sorts of things and assume God applauds such devotion. It's not that He is unimpressed with us at a time like this; He is more interested in how we will be in real life a few days later rather than during our emotional response at church, however sincere we may have been. God tests our earnestness hours, days, or even months later to see how we will react when the divine setup occurs. We may feel this is not very nice for God to do, but does He not have a right to test our promises?

King Saul's downfall came about because he put himself above the revealed word of God during a time of testing. The people were quaking with fear because of the Philistines. Samuel set a time at which he would turn up to offer the burnt offerings. When Samuel did not show up as scheduled, Saul took it upon himself to offer the burnt offering. The Mosaic Law laid down specific instructions that only a priest is authorized to present the burnt offerings (Num. 3:10). But King Saul did it anyway. He explained to Samuel that he felt "compelled" to do it since Samuel turned up too late (1 Sam. 13:11–12).

Saul's claim that he felt compelled to act smacks of the behavior of some people today who fancy that when it comes to the things of God, their feelings are an objective basis on which to operate. Some will even go so far as to say, "The Lord told me to do this," even though the action is blatantly contrary to his own Word! To quote Rob Parsons, Christian men who leave their wives often say such things as: "Darling, we were so young when we got married . . . we didn't really know what we were doing"; "In the long run, this will be better for you"; "This will also turn out to be better for the kids"; or "I've prayed about this, and it's fine with God."

Joseph played hard to get with his eleven brothers when he was prime minister of Egypt. Twenty-two years before they sold him to the Ishmaelites, never expecting to see him again. It was an awful, cowardly thing to do. The time came for these brothers to go to Egypt a second time to buy food, but they did not know they had to face their brother Joseph. He had totally forgiven them in his heart, but now Joseph did something that could be easily misunderstood. When he sent his brothers on their way, he secretly put his cup in Benjamin's bag. Benjamin was then arrested for stealing his cup. On the surface this seems like a cruel joke, yet it was anything but.

It was a setup to see whether the brothers had changed in twenty-two years, to find out if they would do to their brother Benjamin (who had replaced Joseph as his father's favorite son) what they did to Joseph. Here was a perfect opportunity to get rid of Benjamin. When Benjamin was found to have Joseph's cup in his bag the brothers could have said, "Sorry, Benjamin, you are in trouble, you brought this on yourself, and you alone will remain in Egypt to pay for your crime." Instead, they all "tore their clothes," stood by Benjamin, and accompanied him to the prime minister's quarters to plead for mercy.

It was a setup and they passed with flying colors, for they had indeed changed. They were not the same jealous brothers who wanted to get rid of Joseph so many years before. Joseph wept when they pleaded for Benjamin's innocence. At last he revealed his identity to them and also his forgiveness for what they had done twenty-two years before.

Elijah carried out this same tactic of playing hard to get when he put off Elisha's wish for a double portion of his master's anointing—a bold wish (see 2 Kings 2:1–15). On the day Elijah was to be taken away, Elisha doggedly stayed at his master's side. Elijah said to him, "Stay here; the LORD has sent me to Bethel," but Elisha replied, "As surely as the LORD lives and as you live, I will not leave you" (v. 2). Elijah did it again, "Stay here, Elisha; the LORD has sent me to Jericho" (v. 4). But Elisha followed Elijah to Jericho. A third time Elijah tried to put Elisha off, "Stay here; the LORD has sent me to the Jordan" (v. 6). Elisha never left his master's side and was rewarded for his commitment not to let Elijah out of his sight; he received the double portion of Elijah's spirit.

For over ten years I have added this petition to my daily prayer list: *May I recognize the exact moment when God is playing hard to get and never miss his intentions for me.* This teaching has profoundly affected my life and outlook and I predict it will have the same effect on you too.

On the night before Jacob was to be reunited with his brother, Esau, an encounter he was dreading, he found himself wrestling with a man all night long (see Gen. 32:22–26). We won't know the details until we get to heaven, but we do know that at some point during this wrestling match Jacob perceived his opponent was not an enemy after all. Instead, he was wrestling with a highly valued friend who had the power to bless, which Jacob was determined not to miss. God was playing hard to get. Jacob passed the test in what was a pivotal moment for him. Though he might have run away from the stranger at first, Jacob kept struggling with him and eventually got the better of the man—an angel no doubt. He said to Jacob, " 'Let me go, for it is daybreak.' But Jacob replied, 'I will not let you go unless you bless me' " (v. 26). The result: Jacob was given a most wonderful compliment from the Lord—would that God would say such words to me. For the Lord said to Jacob, "You have struggled with God and with men and have overcome" (Gen. 32:28). I love how the King James Version puts it: "For as a prince hast thou power with God and with men, and hast prevailed."

Martin Luther said that you must know God as an enemy before you can know him as a friend. My old friend Rolfe Barnard used to say to people, "Don't tell me when you were saved, tell me when you were lost." Many people assume they were converted because of a profession of faith, but if they do not recall a time when they knew they were lost and in danger of hell, Rolfe reckoned there was reason to question whether their profession of faith is valid.

Arthur Blessitt tells how he was praying at five o'clock in the morning and God told him to take the cross down from the wall in the coffee shop known as His Place on Hollywood's Sunset Strip and carry it around the world. Arthur sometimes speculates, "What if I had stopped praying at four o'clock that morning?" (I had originally assumed he got up early to pray, but it was a case of Arthur praying all night.) One could push this point too far of course, but Arthur's point was that he prayed and prayed and the revelation to start carrying the cross was pivotal in his life.

Closely akin to recognizing God playing hard to get is breaking the betrayal barrier. This is what every sovereign vessel of God sooner or later must do. There comes a time, puzzling though this may be, when God seems to betray those He loves. It is like when God temporarily left Hezekiah or when Martin Luther felt so deserted God seemed like an enemy. God still plays hard to get. Sadly, some people unfamiliar with God's ways walk away and never know the blessing that could be theirs had they persevered in a time of struggling and testing.

Breaking the betrayal barrier is the spiritual equivalent of breaking the sound barrier in aviation. The latter was a great feat, but breaking the betrayal barrier is far more productive for the world because through this experience God takes His seasoned servants and uses them to turn the world upside down.

God told Abraham to leave his own country and come to the land of Canaan. As Stephen recounted in his speech to the Sanhedrin, "He [God] gave him [Abraham] no inheritance here, not even a foot of ground" (Acts 7:5). Abraham must have felt betrayed. And again, when God told him to sacrifice his son Isaac, he must have felt betrayed. When Joseph refused to sleep with Potiphar's wife but was accused of trying to rape her and then slammed into prison—he must have felt betrayed by God. He did the right thing and was punished. When Moses left Pharaoh's palace but was rejected by his fellow Hebrews, he must have felt betrayed. This list goes on and on, and yet the ultimate sense of betrayal rests with our Lord when He cried out on the cross, "My God, my God, why have you forsaken me?" (Matt. 27:46); He must have felt betrayed. All these broke the betrayal barrier, and so can we, but only if we never, never, never give up.

One of the purposes of this book is to show some of God's ways that have been sadly overlooked. We learn God's ways by developing intimacy with Him, by spending time with Him. My wife knows my ways, and I know her ways. Habits. Likes. Dislikes. Predictable responses. God yearned for a people who would know Him so well they would know His ways. Though you may not like this side of Him I have termed "playing hard to get," it is one method by which He communicates. Call it a peculiarity, eccentricity, or strange part of His personality if you like, that is the way He is.

If God accommodates our ill-posed requests He is being too nice. But He can do that too. I have long been gripped by the King James Version rendering of Psalm 106:15: "And he gave them their request; but sent leanness into their soul." Sometimes God gives us what we keep demanding despite His warnings, "This is not best for you"—as when Israel insisted on having a king like other nations. God said to Samuel, "Listen to all that the people are saying to you; it is not you they have rejected, but they have rejected me as their king" (1 Sam. 8:7). God granted their request. Nice God. For a while. But not for long.

James encourages us when he says, "You do not have, because you do not ask God" (Jas. 4:2). I like that! But in the next breath he says, "When you ask, you do not receive, because you ask with wrong motives, that you may spend what you get on your pleasures" (Jas. 4:3). I don't like that. I only wonder to what degree this has applied to me over the years. Is God being nice when He gives us what we want? It would seem so for a time, but not for long.

God is looking for a people who want to know His ways, His heart, and His Word so well that they can learn to pray according to His will. I worry about the spirituality of people (however sincere) who are mostly interested in the "word of knowledge" or the "prophetic word" (or *rhema* word, as it is sometimes called) rather than to know the Bible backward and forward. God hears the prayers of those who pray in His will (1 John 5:14) even if they don't always know they are praying in His will. Paul admitted he did not always know if he was praying in God's will but yielded to the Spirit's infallible intercession which is always in God's will (Rom. 8:26–27). We should keep His will before our eyes whenever we pray because this is what is best for us and what we will never regret.

You can therefore make the case that when God is being nice He really isn't being so nice after all. We will discover at the end of the day that what seemed nice at first wasn't best for us in the long run, that the cost for such niceties eventually becomes too great to bear. God accommodates our comfort zone for a while—when we thought He was being so good to us, but it is only a matter of time before the sobering truth of His playing hard to get is revealed.

The problem is that we hastily assume God is being good to us and answering our prayers and overlooking our superficiality when the truth is that He is instead passing us by. When we are neither hot nor cold but rather lukewarm, we will eventually be spat out of our Lord's mouth (Rev. 3:16). This is the same thing as becoming stone deaf to the Holy Spirit (Heb. 5:13–6:6). Perhaps not today or tomorrow, but it will come.

I therefore use the term "nice" for what often seems nice for a while. Parents may be regarded as nice because they have too few rules, administer very little discipline, or give in to their children's wishes as they grow up. But the cost down the road is incalculable. I used to be so resentful of my parents; they made me go to church it seemed like every time the door was opened, even on Wednesday evenings. I had to stop playing basketball when the kids in the neighborhood played in my own backyard—so I could be hauled off to church. I said, "Daddy, why can't you be nice like Richard's parents?" The parents of the other kids on our block were so nice. (A side note to this discussion—nearly all my old friends who had such nice parents either died early deaths in disgrace or ended up as total failures in life.)

God has given his Word, the Bible, as the road map for the way He wants the Church to glorify Him and the way He wants His children to govern their lives. The slightest deviation from His ways can seem so innocent and innocuous, at first. In the same way, if a jet plane leaving John F. Kennedy airport in New York and heading for London is the slightest degree off course, say only a few miles after takeoff, and if that deviation is not soon corrected, the same plane seven hours later will be circling over Spain rather than Heathrow Airport.

This book is written lovingly and earnestly as what will hopefully be a timely caution to a Church that has generally lost its way. I pray my words do not come across as moralizing or cause any kind of despair or even guilt. Yet if what I write makes sense to you and you feel God is speaking to you, it is a good sign, it seems to me, that God isn't finished with you—there is hope for a bright future.

One way God tests our loyalty and earnestness is to say things we clearly don't understand but which He wants us to believe none the less. This can seem unfair at times. Consider Jesus' words, "Destroy this temple, and I will raise it again in three days" (John 2:19). Who understood these words at the time? Nobody, so far as I know, only the Lord Himself. This might have been a time for some of his followers to say, "Count me out . . . I can't take strange teaching like this." In any case, those very words were used against Jesus later when, at his trial, two men came forward to say, "This fellow said, 'I am able to destroy the temple of God and rebuild it in three days' " (Matt. 26:61).

Take Jesus' words to a mass audience, "I tell you the truth, unless you eat the flesh of the Son of Man and drink his blood, you have no life in you. Whoever eats my flesh and drinks my blood has eternal life" (John 6:53–54). You can't get much more offensive than that. Jesus did not bother to explain what He meant here. He could have said, "Don't worry, this refers to divine communion after I am ascended to heaven," just as He might have said that the destroying and raising of the temple referred to His own body (John 2:21). It was part of the playing hard to get syndrome. Most registered their indignation with comments like, " 'This is a hard teaching. Who can accept it?' . . . And from this time many of his disciples turned back and no longer followed him" (John 6:60–66). For some reason, the Twelve remained. Jesus did ask them, "You do not want to leave too, do you?" (v. 67). Peter replied, "Lord, to whom shall we go? You have the words of eternal life" (v. 68). I doubt the Twelve understood what Jesus meant by eating His flesh and drinking His blood any more than those who turned back, but they stayed with Him.

There are offensive teachings in the Bible, some of which I have chosen to deal with in this book. God wants us to accept His teachings even if we don't understand them. I don't know of anybody who understands the Trinity, Jesus being God and man simultaneously, the power in the blood of Jesus, why God is gracious and just yet lets evil continue, or why He instituted the doctrine of eternal punishment. I'll never forget Mrs. Martyn Lloyd-Jones' observation on the teaching of Hell: "I just go to Genesis 18:25—'Will not the Judge of all the earth do right?' " Some reject what they do not like in Scripture and yet feel God's approval in their comfort zone. God does not disturb them. Not now.

You could say that the central thesis of this book is that there is a sense in which the worst thing that can happen is for God to be nice to us, to let us stay comfortable where we are and never rouse us from our comfort zones. If His being nice means God graciously steps down and rescues us from our blindness and bondage, then may He ever be nice to us. But the worst thing is when He backs away from us, appearing to be nice, and just lets us be. Perhaps in the same way it was said of Ephraim, who was joined to idols: "Leave him alone!" (Hos. 4:17). Those in the Bible who would not accept the revelation of God—whether by creation or through conscience—were not struck down by lightning or brought to their knees by thunder. Instead we read that God merely "gave them over" to their desires and to minds void of judgment (Rom. 1:24, 26, 28).

What is described in Romans 1 does not directly describe the believer but the person who rejects the light of God on their conscience. But this truth is paralleled nonetheless when true believers foolishly say, "I wish God would leave me alone." Be careful or He may do just that. When a believer was sleeping with his stepmother and would not take godly counsel at first, the apostle Paul ordered that man to be handed over to Satan, "so that the sinful nature may be destroyed and his spirit saved on the day of the Lord" (1 Cor. 5:5). Though extreme, we know God can deal with His own people like this. " 'The Lord will judge his people.' It is a dreadful thing to fall into the hands of the living God" (Heb. 10:30–31). I don't want this to happen to you or to me, and yet I want Him to correct me if this is what I need.

·2·

The Comfort Zone

> It is the nature of man as he grows older . . . to protest against change, particularly change for the better.
>
> JOHN STEINBECK

If you read my book *The Anointing* you may recall the chapter entitled "Moving Outside Your Comfort Zone." If you want an increase in your anointing, and if you go where the anointing is to be found, you will almost certainly be required to move outside your comfort zone.

Living in the comfort zone is like being at home with family, with your loved ones. You are at ease, unthreatened. It is familiar because you've been there before. Though it may not be the supernatural peace that transcends understanding promised in Philippians 4:7, it is peaceful nonetheless. It is what I would call natural peace, or peace at the natural level. It simply does not cross your mind to question or be afraid. I grew up in Ashland, Kentucky. It was a town of 29,000 people. I walked to school every day with neighborhood kids who were like family. I didn't realize then of course how precious the days were or how happy I was. A few years ago I took my family back to visit

Ashland. As we drove into the little town, the sign that let us know we were within the city limits said, "Ashland, population 29,000." Forty years later the population count was the same! Seeing that little sign made me feel I was getting back into my comfort zone straight away.

But that feeling ended right there. Nothing else was the same. We drove to my old home on Hilton Avenue. The present owners had changed everything. Even the house next door was altogether different. We drove up and down Hilton Avenue where I had delivered the *Ashland Daily Independent*, our local newspaper, each afternoon when I came home from school. Again, almost all the homes were different. We drove to the school I first attended when I was six years old. It too had changed. The next school where I attended had been torn down. I went to see Coles Junior High but found the building was no longer a school; the same fate was also true for Ashland High School. What used to be the downtown was almost like a ghost town; most shops now reside in a large shopping mall. Even my old church had undergone a face-lift, and the auditorium inside was hardly recognizable.

When I came to Ashland, I wanted to go back home. I couldn't, as the saying goes. After writing most of this chapter Louise and I drove up to Miami from our home in Key Largo to attend the annual Cuba Nostalgia exhibition. Shortly after we married in 1958 we made a couple of trips to Havana, Cuba, and fell in love with that beautiful country as well as certain types of Cuban music. We have owned dozens of records of Cuban music and always enjoy the atmosphere at the exhibition. We drank Cuban coffee, ate Cuban food, enjoyed talking with Cubans who miss their country, and heard Cuban music all over the place. There was nothing spiritual about it—it was wholly nostalgic.

In reflecting on spiritual comfort zones, I often suspect that some people choose a type of ministry, church leader, church, or church service not because it is truly Spirit-filled or theologically sound but rather because it brings a nostalgic feeling of being at home, or what they are used to, or that something they are hoping somehow to recapture. Nostalgia, though we are not always conscious that is what it really is, is perhaps a synonym for "comfort zone." I am perhaps the greatest offender for wanting this.

We continue to try to recapture home, through all different means. I do it with food. I love to eat; it is one of life's greatest pleasures for me. I try to recapture tastes I remember as a child, like the way my grandmother fried chicken or cooked green beans. She went to heaven many years ago and her recipes and way of cooking went with her. Perhaps she cooks for the angels! After marrying, Louise and I used to order a delicious pizza in Fort Lauderdale that far exceeded any I had ever eaten. Sadly, when we were away from Florida that pizza parlor closed and never relocated. And I still long for a pizza like theirs, but it will never happen.

When we made the decision to retire, various friends warned us it would be difficult to settle back into America. "Don't you believe it," I said. Although I knew we would miss England, I was sure it would be good to go home and live in Florida, the land of fishing and sunshine where we lived years before. But, strange as it may seem, we have been out of our comfort zone from the moment we arrived. Nothing is like it had been, other than the good weather. As for fishing, I did more of it when I was minister of Westminster Chapel because we could come to Florida for six weeks each summer and I would do almost nothing but fish. Now that we live in Key Largo, and right on Largo Sound, and even with a little boat waiting for me, for some reason, I do very little fishing. Nothing is like it was.

It is one thing to choose to go outside your comfort zone and quite another to find yourself outside your comfort zone involuntarily. However much you might try to like where you are now or to do what you used to do, you are simply outside your comfort zone.

Being outside your comfort zone is not fun. You are uneasy. You yearn for the familiar. You want what will make you feel good, naturally. Seeking to be within your comfort zone is one of the most natural things in the world to do. And yet if at the natural level you cannot always stay in your comfort zone, how much more is this true at the spiritual level?

As I said, God almost always requires His servants to move outside their comfort zone. Read Hebrews 11, the "faith chapter" of the Bible. A common thread runs through the chapter which characterizes each person's actions being performed by faith; they all had to move outside their comfort zone, and not a single one of them had the luxury of repeating what had been done before them. It is easy to do what has been done before, where there is a precedent for what you are doing; it is safe.

In C. S. Lewis' *The Lion, the Witch and the Wardrobe* are the unforgettable lines:

> "Ooh!" said Susan . . . "Is he—quite safe? I shall feel rather nervous about meeting a lion."
>
> "That you will, dearie, and no mistake," said Mrs. Beaver; "if there's anyone who can appear before Aslan without their knees knocking, they're either braver than most or else just silly."
>
> "Then he isn't safe?" said Lucy.
>
> "Safe?" said Mr. Beaver; "Don't you hear what Mrs. Beaver tells you? Who said anything about safe? 'Course he isn't safe. But he's good. He's the King, I tell you." (Lewis)

God isn't safe. But He's good. We must never forget this when we are outside our comfort zone *yet within God's will.* God wants only what is best for us. When we are directed by the Holy Spirit to be outside our comfort zone, it is always for our good.

For example, Noah "walked with God," following in the steps of Enoch who "walked with God" (Gen. 5:22; 6:9). So far, so good. They both did the same thing. Enoch was taken to heaven one day (Gen. 5:24; Heb. 11:5). As for Noah, he might have wondered each day if he was doing something wrong because though he followed Enoch's example, he was still around! But God had different plans for Noah. He was told one day to build an ark, and with that command came specific instructions (Gen. 6:14ff.). He might have thought: *I'd much prefer to be taken to heaven since I am walking with God as Enoch did.* But he obeyed and "moved with fear" in doing so (Heb. 11:7 KJV), thus putting himself outside his comfort zone. Can you imagine the stigma Noah and his family must have experienced as they constructed that ark—a project unprecedented in history and which must have made them the laughingstock of the people?

Maybe Abraham wondered if he too would get to build an ark, for by this time the idea of building an ark was surely destigmatized since Noah's action had been thoroughly vindicated. Even though God promised He would never again destroy the whole earth by water, building arks nonetheless might have been seen by some as the wave of the future and the evidence you were obedient to God. Noah, however, was the first and last person God required to build an ark.

What if God leads you to do what is unprecedented and which will not be repeated? Can you live with this? Can you accept this? As for Abraham, he found himself outside his comfort zone by not even knowing "where he was going" (Heb. 11:8) or even exactly what he was supposed to do! And what a lackluster legacy he left for Isaac and Jacob; they with Abraham "lived in tents" (Heb. 11:9), hardly the most comfortable way of living.

Moses was brought up in the opposite standard of living of the patriarchs, living in luxury and royal privilege, but he refused to be known as the son of Pharaoh's daughter and "chose to be ill-treated along with the people of God rather than to enjoy the pleasures of sin for a short time" (Heb. 11:24–25). This could not have been an easy decision, but Moses "regarded disgrace for the sake of Christ as of greater value than the treasures of Egypt" (Heb. 11:26). He was definitely living outside his comfort zone.

Hebrews 11:32 refers also to Samuel. He was instructed by God to anoint David to be king when there already was a king. Indeed, Samuel wanted to argue with the Lord on this call: "How can I go? Saul will hear about it and kill me" (1 Sam. 16:2). Yet he had to go where the anointing of the Spirit was present and to find tomorrow's man.

The list in Hebrews 11 goes on and on, even leaving out stalwarts in the Old Testament who could be mentioned. Every single one whom God mightily used, sooner or later, had to move outside their comfort zone. However, all these did what they did voluntarily. They did what they did by faith; they chose to obey the Holy Spirit. Shakespeare said, "Some people are born great, some achieve greatness, and some have greatness thrust upon them." The people described in Hebrews 11 achieved greatness because they willingly went outside their comfort zone. So will you, not necessarily in the eyes of people but in the eyes of Him who will one day look at you and say, "Well done." God wants all of us to experience this.

And yet there is such a thing as having the uneasiness of being outside your comfort zone thrust upon you. It is not what you sought, certainly not what you yearned for. But before you knew it, there it was. Perhaps it was suddenly being in an awkward situation in the office. Maybe you were in an unfamiliar service at church or heard a sermon that made you feel uncomfortable. It may have been an unwelcome knock at your front door. You may have been put on the spot by someone who claimed to be telling you what they thought was for your good. Or perhaps you received unhappy results during a medical examination and your future seems bleak. It isn't fun.

This is not to say, then, that being outside your comfort zone is always and necessarily good. Let no one think that being outside your comfort zone is always a sign of the anointing, or evidence of your obedience, or proof you are pleasing God. It could be the opposite. God has created us with an innate preservation instinct that keeps us from going too close to the edge of a cliff, driving too fast down the freeway, or walking barefoot in an area where there may be snakes and scorpions. I never worried about walking about at night as a boy in Ashland, Kentucky; but I would not feel the same way today, much less walking alone in Miami at night, which is just 50 miles north of where we now live—and some places I wouldn't walk in broad daylight.

We have a natural fear that is God-given; and so we take precautions when we know there could be danger, prepare for an exam when our future is at stake, try to eat less of the wrong foods and more of what we know is healthy. Whereas anxiety may be seen as the common denominator of all psychopathology, there is also an anxiety that can lead to getting things done, referred to as "creative anxiety," which guides one to wonderful inventions and new ideas that change the world for good.

Being outside your comfort zone is not always good—it could be harmful or very bad for you indeed. The devil might even make an overly conscientious person move outside their comfort zone and then cause that person to end up bewildered, disillusioned, depressed, or even in a state of unbelief. I have known some sincere Christians to do foolish things, such as taking their life savings and giving the money away to an unscrupulous preacher; or spending all their time in the work of their church while neglecting their children and letting their marriages break down; or even giving too much time in fasting and prayer only to become weak and tired when they needed to be physically ready and conscientious for their secular jobs.

My favorite line of Shakespeare is: "To thine own self be true." These words are not in the Bible, as far as I know, but the gist of them is found throughout Proverbs and particularly in what Paul is saying in Romans 14, especially verse 9, to which I will return below. I have learned that the Holy Spirit will not lead you to go against Scripture or make you do what gives you an uneasy, unsettled feeling within. Remember throughout the reading of this book this principle that you can hang onto: *The Holy Spirit will never lead you to be untrue to yourself or to violate your conscience.*

The problem is, when you are found outside your comfort zone it is of course unsettling. And if you push this point too far we will all have an excuse to stay in our comfort zones forever. Many things I have had to do over the years to leave my comfort zone made me uneasy at first and were very unsettling indeed.

When I first heard of the Kansas City Prophets (as they were then called), I hit the ceiling! Not only did these men take me out of my comfort zone, I found myself in the "alarm bells" zone. The more I heard in those early days, the more I felt I must roll up my sleeves and warn my friends about these occultists. Talk about being outside my comfort zone! But I was wrong. In a few months I climbed down and found myself having to make a hard decision—whether or not to be involved with some of them. One or two became close friends. I have been thankful ever since. But I was outside my comfort zone, at first.

What is outside your comfort zone today may be at the very center of your comfort zone tomorrow. This is because once you obey and become used to the scariness of your new place, being outside your comfort zone begins to seem like home. Before long you may have to move yet again and go to the unknown, like Abraham who went out but did not know where he was going.

Whether it be an unusual ministry or a different theological point of view, an initial uneasiness is what we all tend to feel when we are outside our comfort zone. We can choose to say "This is like walking the streets of Miami at night" and stay away, or we can ask ourselves whether the Holy Spirit could be leading us on to a greater anointing of the Spirit than we have ever known in our lives.

P–E–A–C–E

How then do we know we are outside our comfort zone but still in God's perfect will? I will now share an acrostic that has served me well over the years and one which I have shared with the members of Westminster Chapel many times—both from the pulpit and in the vestry. It is based upon an acrostic, P–E–A–C–E. Consider asking these questions when you are not sure what to do.

Providential

Is it providential? Do things happen or do you have to break a door down in order to get through it? If you have to force a door open or nudge the arm of Providence, be careful: You are about to enter a realm outside your comfort zone, yes, but not a realm that is accompanied by the peace of God. If things happen without your manipulation, proceed, but if you have played 'man the manipulator' and made things happen to suit your wishes, *stop*. God almost certainly is not behind what you are trying to do.

Enemy

What would your enemy—the devil—want you to do? I often ask myself what Satan would want me to do at this point. Figure that out (it probably won't be very hard) and do the opposite. Most of us have a fairly shrewd idea what the devil would want us to do: cheat, hate, have sex outside of marriage, go deeply into debt, boast about our accomplishments, act jealous, gossip, point the finger, hold a grudge. Do the opposite and you will almost certainly get it right.

Authority

What does the Bible say? The Bible is your supreme and infallible authority for faith and conduct. You will never improve on Holy Scripture. The way to know the will of God begins with knowing the Bible well. It is entirely God-breathed (2 Tim. 3:16) and therefore written by the Holy Spirit (2 Pet. 1:21). You should ask whether there is a biblical warrant for what you are thinking of doing or embracing. If it is not validated by Scripture, *stop* at once. No need to proceed to the next premise. God will never lead you to do that which clearly goes against His own Word.

Confidence

Am I confident this is the will of God for me? When I am the most sure I am in the will of God, I am the most confident. When I know I am obedient, that I am doing what I have a mandate to do, I feel confident through and through. A Greek word for this is *parresia*, which means "boldness." Sometimes translated as "plainly" (John 10:24), it is what Peter experienced when he preached on the day of Pentecost (Acts 2:29). It is a good, good feeling, and when I lose this it is often a signal to me that something has gone wrong. God wants you to feel confident.

Ease

In your heart of hearts do you feel at ease? Are you troubled or unsettled? Be very, very careful. From my own experience, if I have peace inside, even when I am scared and conscious that I am making a hard decision, I am seldom disappointed when I proceed. When we announced my decision to retire from Westminster Chapel, having been there for twenty-five years, I had times of near panic when I did wonder what I was doing. Yet even as I was giving up security and leaving when others were begging me to stay, I had peace in my heart of hearts.

For this acrostic to be a safe guide for you, all five of these points must come together. If only four are true in your case, that is still not enough. To have peace we need all of them. Indeed, if all five are there, I can safely promise you it will be a positive and happy journey forward.

I now come to Romans 14:19, the foundational verse for my P–E–A–C–E acrostic above. Paul says, "Let us therefore make every effort to do what leads to peace and to mutual edification" (Rom. 14:19). The peace I have in mind in the above acrostic is internal, the ease we feel within, but Paul also has in mind what leads to peace with others. Previously he said: "If it is possible, as far as it depends on you, live at peace with everyone" (Rom. 12:18). We will always have those who do not want to make peace with us, but we must try.

The question we now must attempt to answer is: How do you know when being outside your comfort zone is of the Holy Spirit and when it is your own doing? In my book *The Anointing* I have a chapter entitled "The Limits of Our Anointing" where I make the case that we all must accept the limits of our anointing. Nobody can do everything. King Saul's downfall began when he went outside his anointing. As we saw above, because he was king he thought he was above the Word of God and also could go outside his calling, including offering the burnt offering—an act only a priest was allowed to do. But Saul did just that, only to be told by Samuel that "You acted foolishly." Samuel then prophesied that Saul would be replaced by a man after God's own heart (1 Sam. 13:9–14).

It takes a lot of humility (and sometimes courage) to recognize the limits of your anointing and never to go outside that anointing. This principle is based partly on Romans 12:3: "Do not think of yourself more highly than you ought, but rather think of yourself with sober judgment, in accordance with the measure of faith God has given you." I have to accept the limits of my intelligence, gifting, and calling. I must not try to be somebody else or imitate another's gift or anointing. God made only one you and then He threw the mold away. He wants each of us to accept ourselves as we are and to be content with the way He made us and with our particular calling.

King Saul wasn't content with his calling. You would have thought that being king would be enough! No. He wanted more. He took himself too seriously and it led to his downfall. We therefore must accept the limits of our gifting but also our mandate. We must not transgress by crossing over a line by which we go outside that calling.

I have been given an opportunity to talk with certain leaders in the Middle East, among them the late Yasser Arafat. It is an honor to be invited into the presence of a head of state and have lunch with them, regardless whether you agree with everything for which they stand. But political leaders, understandably, want to talk politics. I made it clear to Arafat that my role is theological and non-political. I said to him: "I do not come to you as a political leader but as a follower of Jesus Christ. I come as a man of prayer." Sitting around that long table in Ramallah, the Palestinian leaders would still bring up political issues, but I forced myself to avoid delving into politics and instead live within my calling: to pray and talk about Jesus Christ.

The funny thing is, going into politics with Israeli and Palestinian leaders would be widening my comfort zone. I happen to love politics. Ninety percent of my television watching involves political news. I have some fairly strong political views, but I do not make them public, or even private if I think somebody might quote me. Therefore to concentrate on politics would be right in the middle of my comfort zone. To avoid politics, however, especially if I can please those around me when I am with political leaders, is to go outside my comfort zone—which I am required to do.

The irony is, staying with your calling is in a sense to stay in your comfort zone because this is where you have maximum peace. Yet the time will come sooner or later when you must go outside your comfort zone to keep that peace, but never outside your calling. So how do I know when I am being cautious and prudent by refusing to be found outside my comfort zone? How do I know when it is a natural but reasonable fear that keeps me where I am? How do I know this fear is not a fear of displeasing the Lord? There is one answer: *When pride is at stake*. Commonly called "the fear of man"—the fear of what people will think or say—this is precisely what keeps us in our comfort zone and thus mitigates against our discovering God's ways.

These words keep coming back to me: "They have not known my ways" (Ps. 95:10; Heb. 3:10), stated in anger but nonetheless with lament and sorrow. God's heart ached when he said, "I was grieved with that generation"; namely, that ancient generation of Israel that might have inherited the Promised Land but forfeited it. This is the way God feels about us when we shrink back and reject the offer He makes to us, the way He has revealed himself to us, and the things He has asked us to do. He wants us to know His ways. He yearns for us to know what He is like and love Him for being just as He is.

The greatest sentiment one's husband or wife wants to receive from the other is to be loved just the way you are. It is so affirming to be fully accepted as we are. God wants that from us. He wants us to know Him, to see exactly what He is like, to know what He calls "my ways." The thing is, you might not like His ways. You may dislike His ways intensely, for all I know. But the point is, God wants us to know His ways and love Him just as He is. The problem with Israel was this people did not even know His ways. This made God sad but also angry.

God wants us to know Him so well that what He does no longer takes us by surprise. For those who do not know His ways a reaction follows; they will say "This cannot be God" when He chooses to manifest Himself in a manner that finds us outside our comfort zone.

Is your mind made up as to what God is like? Is your perception of God a projection or the real picture? We must have courage to overcome our fears and thus explore the awesome things about God that He wants to show us. This book is designed to warn us and, if possible, to catch us in time so that we will discover before it is too late what God wants us to see about Him. We need not be like the comfortable majority who opt for the familiar.

The question is: When is it a black or white situation (to sin or not to sin) and when is it a gray-area situation—when you are not displeasing God? *When God clearly calls you to move outside your comfort zone*—as He did with Noah, Abraham, Moses, and Samuel. When God clearly taps you on the shoulder then move is what you and I must do; we have no choice but to obey. Otherwise we forfeit the blessing of the Holy Spirit and risk the unthinkable—not hearing God speak to us again and becoming stone deaf to the Holy Spirit (Heb. 5:11–6:6). I faced a hard decision shortly after Arthur Blessitt visited us at Westminster Chapel in 1982. My options were to continue what he started (chorus singing, the altar call, and witnessing on the streets) or go back to business as usual. I also had to decide whether I was being led by the Holy Spirit to mold Westminster Chapel into a charismatic church. Some might think we did become a charismatic church back then, though I maintain we did not. The proof of this rests in the fact that I had many charismatic leaders whom I greatly respected urging me to press on with what we began. The big question those days was whether I was taking the chapel too fast, slow, or just right. I was under some pressure to do things "charismatic," but I never felt right about it as I had no mandate from the Holy Spirit.

To some in the church, what was begun under Arthur's influence seemed very charismatic. Yet pressing on with a certain style and exercising all the gifts of the Spirit in the services would take us even farther outside our comfort zone, which some in the congregation pleaded with me to do. I did not follow their advice. We went at our own pace, and some thought we moved too fast, some not fast enough.

I chose a comfort zone this time. We kept at a pace that, it seemed to me, was right for our people who by and large had no background whatsoever in things charismatic, only reformed thinking. You might say I gave in to a weakness as I did not want to displease certain people more than I had already. (I barely kept the old battleship afloat as it was!) And yet some have lovingly argued with me that I would have done far better to ignore all critics and followers and just went for it, regardless of the consequences. Though I could have, and I would have done it to glorify God, I just did not have the intestinal fortitude to do so. I gave in to a weakness, but I do not believe I sinned.

Did Moses sin when he gave in to the people to allow divorce? See Deuteronomy 24:1–4. Jesus said that Moses "permitted you to divorce your wives because your hearts were hard. But it was not this way from the beginning" (Matt. 19:8). Those words "it was not this way from the beginning" indicate Moses would have been quite right never to allow divorce. But he gave in to the people. Was this Moses' comfort zone? I think it could have been. Did he sin by giving in to them? No. He apparently did this without displeasing God. And yet I think too that God was being nice.

I can recall other situations in Westminster Chapel when I opted for the comfort zone out of weakness; several occurrences emerged in my final year to which I will refer. I announced my retirement thirteen months in advance to give the chapel time to make the transition after having me since 1977. I still hoped revival would come during the final year—I took a lot of risks but also gave in to a weakness, twice.

The first of these was when I found out that Mahesh Chavda was free to hold an all-night prayer meeting for us at Westminster Chapel. This had been an aspiration of mine ever since some of our people, including Louise, attended one of Mahesh's all-night prayer meetings in west London. I was so thrilled he was able to commit his time to our church. I took advantage of it with both hands and announced the news publicly. Many were as thrilled as I. The next day, however, our chapel manager told me we could not hold this all-night meeting as he had recently sent out a letter to the surrounding neighbors of the chapel promising we would no longer hold services after ten o'clock at night. This came about because neighbors had complained about loud music late one Saturday evening when a certain charismatic group of people had asked to use the chapel for the day. Our manager wanted to keep his promise that this would not happen again.

I could have overruled his decision; I had not written the letter and had not asked him to write it, although what he did was a reasonable response. I could have said, "Sorry, but I already promised Mahesh and the people we will do this. Besides, we want to be open to the Holy Spirit and pray for revival." I could have just let the neighbors complain again, or I could have asked the people who attended the all-night prayer meeting to be as quiet as possible—although it is fairly certain we would have been heard in the wee hours of the morning. I gave in and yielded to a comfort zone. I did not want to offend anybody in my final year at the chapel. I phoned Mahesh, who graciously accepted my apology. But I have wondered many times what might have happened had we proceeded with that all-night prayer meeting.

Another incident happened toward the end of my service at Westminster, one I have worried more over. I began an era of spontaneous singing at the chapel during the partaking of the Lord's Supper. Usually after the bread and wine were served to those present, I began singing—making up the words as we went along: "We praise you, Lord . . . we love your name . . . we honor you . . . welcome, Holy Spirit . . ." This was done without any musical accompaniment and yet we sang on key together. The sound was glorious as the congregation joined in. Sometimes during these moments, the Spirit would come down in great power. People would laugh, or groan. Some would fall off the pews and onto the floor. It was one of the most memorable eras of my whole twenty-five years at Westminster Chapel, but some in the church were not pleased. And as a result, I gave in rather than allow for the possibility of a big blowup just before retiring.

Again, I do not believe I sinned in either of these incidents, but I did give in to weakness nonetheless. I am not thrilled with my decisions. I like to think, just maybe, it was comparable to Paul escaping from the Damascenes—an event he called a weakness (2 Cor. 11:30–33). He was not thrilled with what he did either.

There is one further aspect to the comfort zone syndrome which I must address in this chapter. I refer now to the way our perception of a comfort zone changes according to our being either "in season" or "out of season." "In season" is when the full tide of a spiritual wave has set in and powerfully washes away or hides the debris that was visible on the shoreline. When the Holy Spirit is present in power, things do not tend to bother, upset, or even threaten us as they did before. The Spirit makes our problems disappear!

When I first had the vision of the Pilot Light ministry which led to our street witnessing, nothing could have stopped me from being out on the steps of the chapel to witness to passersby that first Saturday in June 1982. I would have done it alone. Several volunteers joined me, but I was so full of assurance of the Spirit—I had a rugged boldness and freedom I had not known before—that I would have gladly appeared by myself and handed out tracts while talking to people about Jesus Christ.

But a year or two later the tide began to ebb, and another "out of season" moment was born. Our excitement diminished. Many who had started out with us stopped coming on Saturday mornings. The number of people praying to receive Christ dropped to nearly zero, week after week. Now I didn't feel like coming. I felt I could use these Saturdays to better advantage. When I first started the work with Arthur I was out of my comfort zone. But in a short period of time I was at home with this, full of confidence, and with a sense of God on me. But I realized later that I was now out of my comfort zone again. Nothing came to fruition as I had hoped—revival certainly had not come. We were not reaching many people that we knew of. To remain a Pilot Light and keep that ministry going meant again extending outside my comfort zone. I eventually experienced four stages:

1. Out of my comfort zone (when I first started witnessing on the streets).
2. In my comfort zone (once I powerfully felt the Lord with me).
3. Out of my comfort zone (when I realized nothing great was happening as a result of our faithful witnessing every Saturday).
4. Out of my comfort zone but committed to the ministry. Whether many joined me or if people were converted was irrelevant. I showed up every Saturday to keep the Pilot Light ministry going.

A few years later, a gentleman by the name of Benjamin Chan started a prayer meeting on Saturday mornings to uphold us before the Lord while we were evangelizing on the streets. We did not do one thing differently, but we noticed a dramatic increase in the number of people who prayed to receive Christ. The Pilot Light ministry began to flourish and continues to this day. I never missed a Saturday during the final twenty years of my London ministry unless I was out of town.

My point is this: When the Spirit subsides and ebb tide comes, we find ourselves outside our comfort zone again. This is because the Holy Spirit at first makes us comfortable in the very sphere we once dreaded. But then He tests us to see what we will do during ebb tide. This is why Paul admonished that we be "instant" whether in season or out of season (2 Tim. 4:2 KJV). Therefore when there is a diminishing in the measure of the Spirit's assurance and comfort, and the tide goes out, the debris and all sorts of things that were on the shoreline yet covered over become obvious, and obstacles loom large. We then must make the choice to please God by doing what we know is right even if we don't feel like doing it—whether by spending time in prayer, reading the Bible every day, witnessing, tithing, or any number of other activities which can become tedious and boring, if not sheer drudgery, when God hides his face.

When the tide is in it is easier to do the things we know we ought to do. In those seasons it isn't so hard to practice total forgiveness, dignifying the trial, witnessing to the lost, turning the other cheek (Matt. 5:39), accepting an injustice (1 Cor. 6:7), or not taking oneself so seriously. The problem with the old spiritual's premise, "Every time I feel the Spirit moving in my heart I'll pray," is that when the Spirit is moving in your heart it is warm, comfortable, and like the comfort zone! Then it is easy to pray and do what is required of us.

True spirituality is present when you don't feel the Spirit moving in your heart and you pray anyway. When you carry out obedience even when you do not feel like doing it, you are venturing outside your comfort zone. This pleases God and honors Him to no end. The Holy Spirit is depicted in the New Testament as a dove, a very shy, sensitive bird. Pigeons and doves are in the same family but they are nonetheless quite different birds. Doves are gentle, peaceable birds yet afraid of people and easily scared away. When Paul said, "Do not grieve the Holy Spirit of God" (Eph. 4:30), he used a word that in the Greek means "to get your feelings hurt." The Holy Spirit, a very sensitive person, gets His feelings hurt easily, but never lets on that He is offended. When the Dove lifts from us we don't feel a thing. We just carry on as if nothing happened, often not realizing until much later that we have offended the Spirit. Consider the oft-repeated statement, "If the Holy Spirit were completely withdrawn from the Church today, ninety percent of the work of the Church would continue on as if nothing happened."

In much the same way the Holy Spirit flutters away and leaves us to ourselves and we continue without Him, like Joseph and Mary, who went a day's journey without Jesus, thinking He was right there with them (Luke 2:43–44). It is scary to realize that this continues to happen. God unobtrusively slips away from us and we feel nothing while often thinking the Lord is with us as much as ever. We become accustomed to an existence without His powerful, conscious presence; we begin to assume we are still being led by Him.

Now to what is perhaps the most important point yet. For whatever reason, when the Spirit is not powerfully present, the tide is out. We tend to make critical decisions in that state which are dictated by the flesh and not the Spirit, even though we may think it is the Spirit directing us. And because the Holy Spirit tends to diminish in small measure like the ebbing tide, and not all at once, we move back into the old comfort zone and do not realize we are vulnerable to fleshly decisions, to choices we would not make were we filled with the Spirit.

For example, once we make the decision to forgive someone totally, it is an act of our will, and yet it is done through the supernatural power of the Holy Spirit. Later we often begin to say to ourselves, "It isn't right that this person I have forgiven is going to walk away and not be caught or found out." We get upset, and if we are not careful we slip into the old comfort zone that justifies the anger and the grudge. What are we to do? There is only one answer: Move outside your comfort zone again and forgive them.

But when the Spirit wanes, and He usually does, we are liable to make fleshly decisions. At the time we think our judgments are sound, solid, and spiritual, but they may not be at all. And in regard to total forgiveness, it is one of the hardest things in the world to maintain. "The heart is deceitful above all things, and desperately wicked: who can know it?" (Jer. 17:9 KJV). If we are not careful, we begin holding a grudge all over again against the very people we forgave before.

So too with the way we react to a manifestation of the Holy Spirit. When we are full of the Spirit and walking in the Spirit we will not miss what God is doing when the Spirit manifests—whether through crying or laughing or falling on the floor. But when we are in the flesh we find this sort of thing irritating and reprehensible . . . and fancy we have spiritual discernment! I know, I've been there!

Many of us miss what God is doing because we fancy ourselves to be competent, spiritual judges of what is happening when in fact we may have become lukewarm and smug. Our comfort zones can masquerade as the witness of the Spirit when it is really a case of the tide being out and our having very little authentic discernment. When we are in this state God is nice, at least for a while. He lets us do what we want to do. We may later question why God let us stay like that, or why He didn't open our eyes. The answer comes with the niceness of God painlessly letting us off the hook and moving on without us when we didn't pick up on his subtle wooing. He leaves us alone when we are smug and unteachable. Perhaps He waits for a time we will be in a fit state to listen to Him. It is when the tide is fully in, and when it is in season with us, that we can grasp what He is like and love Him for being the way He is. It is the way we would see things were we to leave our comfort zones purely out of obedience and for His glory.

If what follows in this book causes offense, note that it may be blindness that keeps you comfortable in that state rather than the way you would see things were you wide awake and keeping in step with the Holy Spirit. Or, dare I say it, the way we will all see things one day.

If you are spiritually asleep like the foolish virgins (Matt. 25:1–5), please wake up, although you will probably not like a lot of what follows in this book. There are three things you probably already know about sleep:

1. We don't know we are asleep until we wake up.
2. We do things in our dreams we would not do wide awake.
3. We hate the sound of an alarm.

This book is designed to help us see for ourselves whether our comfort zone is a benign gray area or if it is a case of God graciously arousing us from slumber. Let your perception of Nice God shift to seeing the one true God of the Bible. If He so arouses us He is being more than nice—indeed He is awesome and merciful too.

May the Holy Spirit guide us as we take a look at the true God. He's not safe, but he is good. Moreover, this can be the crucial test whether God means more to you and me than anything or anyone else.

· 3 ·

The Fear and Jealousy of God

> I don't think anything has been done in the name of Christ and under the banner of Christianity that has proven more destructive to human personality, and hence counterproductive to the evangelistic enterprise, than the un-Christian, uncouth strategy of attempting to make people aware of their lost and sinful condition.
>
> A POPULAR AMERICAN TELEVISION PASTOR

I had a head start when it comes to the knowledge of the fear and jealousy of God. My old church in Ashland, Kentucky, was begun during the tail end of America's Second Great Awakening in the 1840s. The Cane Ridge Revival had erupted in Kentucky in 1801 and spread Christianity all over my old state and much of the South as well. People came in their covered wagons to Bourbon County, Kentucky, for preaching and fellowship. It was the start of the "camp meeting" phenomenon. According to one eyewitness account, people were falling down (something new among Presbyterians). Congregants were astonished, but curious, particularly when people fell during the most solemn parts of divine service . . . [at one point] no less than 1,000 people fell prostrate to the ground, including many infidels. These persons falling down were carried out of the crowd by those next to them, and taken to some convenient place, where others prayed over them.

Those who fell down were said to be "totally powerless" just before they fell. Others not so overcome were simply "unable to stand or sit" but had the "use of their hands and could converse with perfect composure." In some cases they were "unable to speak, their pulses became weak, and they drew a difficult breath about once a minute." For yet others, "all signs of life forsook them for nearly an hour." Once they recovered they felt no bodily pain, "had the entire use of their reason" and could even "relate everything that had been said or done near them."

One participant in the Cane Ridge revival told how, having no invitation to speak, he decided to preach anyway by using "the body of a fallen tree" to stand on. He stated that he commenced reading a hymn with an audible voice, and by the time they concluded singing and praying, they had around them, standing on their feet, approximately 10,000 people. He says he gave out his text . . . "For we must all stand before the judgment seat of Christ" and before concluding, his voice was not to be heard over groans of distress and shouts of triumph. Hundreds fell prostrate to the ground, and the work of conversion continued there until Wednesday afternoon. Some estimated that at least 500 were lying on the ground together in deepest agonies, and then every few minutes were rising in shouts of triumph.

The "sound of Niagara" was how the noise was described as their voices could be heard a mile away. This sort of atmosphere swept into the South and by the early twentieth century represented the norm in many churches, including mine.

I was brought up in the Church of the Nazarene; in my town we were nicknamed "Noisyrenes." Our shouts of praise, however, were paralleled by a great sense of the fear of God through much of the preaching. The man who may be mostly responsible for my early conversion and spiritual development, other than my father, was Rev. Gene Phillips. His preaching was absolutely awesome and unforgettable, and engendered such a sense of the fear of God in me that I never outgrew it. This is why I said I had a head start on the subject of this chapter.

The next pastor who came to Ashland was Rev. Harold Daniels. He invited Rev. W. M. Tidwell, age eighty, to hold a series of services that lasted two weeks. I was only about fifteen years old but I remember very clearly one service that characterized rather well how his teaching was used to bring a great sense of the fear of God to settle on the congregation; that is, everyone except for one girl named Patsy. My mother always sat near the front of the church, but for some reason she was in the back of the auditorium that morning; hence she was able to witness Patsy's very poor attitude and behavior that morning.

Tidwell was a bit eccentric in his preaching and actually used me for a sermon illustration that morning as he preached on the parable of the wedding garment. His text was from Matthew 22:11–13:

> But when the king came in to see the guests, he noticed a man there who was not wearing wedding clothes. "Friend," he [the king] asked, "how did you get in here without wedding clothes?" The man was speechless. Then the king told the attendants, "Tie him hand and foot, and throw him outside, into the darkness, where there will be weeping and gnashing of teeth."

At the appropriate moment in the sermon, I would be summoned to the front and asked, "Why do you not have the wedding garment?" I would appear speechless and then be bound hand and foot by four of the men in the congregation who were ordered to take me out of the church building, symbolizing the outer darkness.

Patsy laughed and scoffed throughout the entire service and showed open irreverence. Many in the congregation were worried about her at the time she did this. She snickered as the four men carried me out of the church by the center aisle, right past where she was seated on the back row.

Dr. Tidwell gave the altar call, and some people responded. He stopped the singing at one point during the invitational hymn to say, "Someone here this morning is getting their last call. If you do not come to the Lord this morning, you will never again have an opportunity to be saved." I myself have never said this in a service in my fifty years of preaching, and I have never known anybody else to do it either. But Rev. Tidwell did.

He then turned to Pastor Daniels and said, "I will not close this service, I will turn it over to you." Pastor Daniels said he would not close it either and sat down. When Rev. Tidwell said that someone was getting their last call, some people, including my mother, actually wondered if he was referring to Patsy, though it seemed unlikely given she was so young. Slowly people got up to leave, including Patsy. She did not return to the church service that evening.

The next day, Patsy was killed as she was walking home from school. What happened was a car missed a stop (the stop sign had been turned around by some mischievous kids) and hit another car, pushing it wildly onto the sidewalk right where Patsy was walking. She was killed instantly.

In those days I was responsible for delivering the local newspaper, the *Ashland Daily Independent*, to about 110 homes each day after I came home from school. When I finished my rounds and returned home, my mother met me on the front porch, crying. "Have you heard about Patsy?" she asked.

"No, what do you mean?"

Sobbing between breaths my mother said, "She was just killed by a car a few moments ago as she was walking home from school."

I was sobered from the crown of my head to the soles of my feet. I was gutted as I had never been in my life. I never again passed by 25th Street and Montgomery Avenue without remembering that incident. When I was in Ashland last summer I even drove Louise by to show her the spot.

The effect that moment had on me has never left. It instilled into me to the utter depths of my soul a sense of the fear of God and the importance of obeying the Holy Spirit. We must not forget the need to be saved before it is eternally too late. When the Holy Spirit said, "Today, if you hear his voice, do not harden your hearts . . ." (Ps. 95:7-8), He really did mean it. People need to be saved or they will be everlastingly lost.

One can sympathize somewhat with the quotation at the beginning of this chapter. The use of manipulation in evangelism for the purpose of scaring people is not to be condoned. I have seen enough of this in my old denomination too. Only the Holy Spirit can make a person see their lost condition, but should the Holy Spirit Himself choose to intervene and take over and lead a minister to say what Rev. Tidwell said, it could be seen as manipulation, or even what one might call destructive and counterproductive preaching.

However, I conclude that Rev. Tidwell's words were not a manipulative ploy at all; the atmosphere of the fear of God, combined with the horrible event of the following day, serve as evidence that God was graciously warning Patsy and many other people of their eternal state. Yet it wasn't very nice.

Our Pilot Light ministry in London, ministered on the streets near Buckingham Gate and Victoria, continued nonstop (save for Christmas and Boxing Day) for the last twenty years I was at Westminster Chapel. The gospel has been presented to thousands, and hundreds have made professions. But were they all saved? I know some were and suspect many more were converted (at the time or eventually) than we realized.

On one of the last days I served that ministry, I gave a tract translated into German to a young man. A few months later, after our retirement, a letter came from him in Germany. He said he had been praying for his father for years and years with no apparent success. But he had given the tract to his dad and was writing to say his father received Christ as his Lord and Savior as a result of reading it. The convicted man died suddenly the next day. It was a poignant reminder for the importance of never missing an opportunity to witness—the listener may never hear the gospel again. I used to urge Pilot Lights to present the gospel "as though their destiny were in their hands and yours because they may never hear the gospel again."

We live in what Dr. O. S. Hawkins calls "the No Fear culture." O. S. suggests it is because "our generation knows little of the nature of God." People in and out of the Church have no fear of God. He defines the fear of God as being "a reverential awe, a sense of being afraid of offending a holy God in any way." I am thankful he is not afraid to use the word "afraid." So many water down the fear of God by quickly saying, "Now that doesn't mean to be afraid of God." Really? It certainly does mean that; otherwise nobody will begin to feel real respect and awe for the God of the Bible. When the Bible refers to people walking in the fear of the Lord, I believe it means that they were in fact scared to death.

The fear of God is a no-nonsense and no-joke reality. It is

very real when described in the Bible and is often intended to strike fear in us—even shake us to our fingertips. It did in the early Church, following what characterized the atmosphere during Jesus' ministry when he performed miracles and when the apostles preached the gospel. Many modern versions translate the Greek word *phobos* as "awe," which of course it is. Yet "awe" does not always mediate the feeling the writers intended when they used *phobos* (from which we get the suffix "phobia"). The first time the word "fear" appears in the New Testament is when the angel said to Joseph, "Fear not to take unto thee Mary thy wife" (Matt. 1:20 KJV). Clearly the writer did not mean, "Do not be in awe." The NIV rightly translates this phrase, "Do not be afraid." Yet not using the word "fear" in so many instances could somehow make many miss the actual feeling the writer wanted to convey. This confusion is due partly to the fact that the word "awe" can also mean admiration, and the word "awesome" today can mean even "incredible" or "cool."

I am confident that all who were present when Jesus healed the paralyzed man who was presented through the roof glorified God and "were filled with fear" (Luke 5:26 KJV). When a boy was raised from the dead, "there came a fear on all" (Luke 7:16 KJV). When the residents in the country of the Gadarenes urged Jesus to leave the area because the demon-possessed man had been miraculously delivered it was because "they were taken with great fear" (Luke 8:37 KJV).

This theme continues in the book of Acts. One forgotten fallout of the happenings on the day of Pentecost was that "fear came upon every soul" (Acts 2:43 KJV). When Ananias was struck dead for lying to the Holy Spirit, "great fear came on all" (Acts 5:5 KJV), as was the case shortly after, when the same thing happened to Sapphira and "great fear came upon all the church" (Acts 5:11 KJV). Later on, when Saul of Tarsus was converted, the church had an era of rest and peace and yet they were still "walking in the fear of the Lord" (Acts 9:31 KJV).

When the sons of Sceva failed in their attempt to cast out demons but were overcome by them, the result was that "fear fell on them all, and the name of the Lord Jesus was magnified" (Acts 19:17 KJV). Paul said, "Them that sin rebuke before all, that others also may fear" (1 Tim. 5:20 KJV). Noah "moved with fear" in his obedience to God (Heb. 11:7 KJV). The effect of the lightning and thunder at Mount Sinai caused Moses to say "I exceedingly fear and quake" (Heb. 12:21 KJV). We are commanded to serve God with "reverence and godly fear" (Heb. 12:28 KJV). Peter admonished us to "pass the time of your sojourning here in fear" (1 Pet. 1:17 KJV).

This is to take absolutely nothing from the fact that the earliest Church equally and simultaneously experienced great joy. The same disciples who were filled with fear were equally "filled with joy" (Acts 13:52). When people saw the miraculous in Samaria there was "great joy" there (Acts 8:8). Similarly, the news of Gentiles being converted resulted in "great joy" (Acts 15:3 KJV). It is entirely possible to feel joy and fear simultaneously: When Jesus was raised from the dead the women who heard the report from the angels were both "afraid yet filled with joy" (Matt. 28:8).

The first message of the New Testament was directed to Pharisees and Sadducees—to "flee from the coming wrath" (Matt. 3:7). Why would a person flee, meaning "run"? To grasp the meaning of John the Baptist's message meant these men were to be afraid of the coming wrath. They could not just politely tip their heads toward God or show a bit of respectful deference; instead, they were told to be fearful of what was coming. It is my view that the coming revival will usher in simultaneous fear and joy to the people. It will send terror to the lost and backsliders and bring both fear and joy to those walking in the light.

What does walking in the fear of the Lord mean? It certainly does mean to worship with reverence and awe, but it also means to live in fear of displeasing the Lord. I realize there are always those people (and every pastor faces this) who are overly conscientious—almost to the point of being neurotic—when this kind of teaching is carried out. Understand, I certainly do not want to add to anyone's anxiety unnecessarily in these lines. Let me explain what I mean.

A deep and true fear of God will keep you from committing adultery because of what it does to God, the Church, the one you would be involved with, your spouse, family, and you. To have a fear of God will mean that we are afraid to kill anybody for the same reasons. When we develop a sensitivity to the Holy Spirit, we are equally afraid to commit adultery in our *heart*, or to hurt another person's *reputation* with gossip, or to hold a *grudge*, or to do anything that might bring vengeance. The Sermon on the Mount was given to develop a true fear of the Lord, shown by the way we live.

The Holy Spirit mirrors the God of the Bible and is as sensitive to what displeases the Father as the Father Himself. Therefore when we develop a care not to grieve the Holy Spirit we do not act in a manner we know would bring Him displeasure. A healthy Christian fears God's chastening and disciplining. Said the psalmist, "O LORD, do not rebuke me in your anger or discipline me in your wrath." The King James Version translates this same verse as "hot displeasure." The reason God disciplines us is because of His jealous love.

John 5:44 is the verse I seek to have govern me more than any other. I was initially influenced by the King James Version:

"How can ye believe, which receive honour one of another, and seek not the honour that cometh from God only?" This translation stresses the honor that only God—not people—is prepared to bestow, that we should seek His pleasure and approval alone. Most versions translate "from God only" as "the only God," which does not change the aforementioned meaning. However, if there is a blessing that comes from seeking only His approval and not the affirmation of each other, this, I for one want.

John 5:44 assumes that God is jealous. He doesn't like it when we opt for human approval rather than His alone. This is exactly what the ancient Jews did; it is the precise reason they missed their own Messiah when he came. When Jesus stood before the Jews and they rejected Him, He told them why they were blind: it is because they seek honor from one another and that they did not seek the honor that comes from the only true God. Had they been seeking His honor instead of each other's they would have recognized the One God sent to them. Hence Jesus asked, "How can you believe [in other words, *You are not able to believe*] when you do not make any real attempt to receive the honor that comes from God alone?"

When we seek His honor over the approval of people, God rewards us—whether with vindication, other good gifts, or with insight; when we seek the approval of people instead, God's jealousy sets in and He withholds such blessings, including insight. This is what happened to ancient Israel in Jesus' day. They knew He was a jealous God, but they let pride rule, wanting approval of each other and not what God wanted to give them.

This principle still applies. John 5:44 is one of those verses that grips me to such depths I am often overcome with godly fear. I have wanted to write a book on this verse more than anything else in the world. The only reason I have not written a book on this is that God won't show me more about this verse than I need to know. It could be that my own desire to write such a book is of the flesh and an unconscious desire to get the applause of people for writing such a book. God Himself withholds the further insight I need. I only know that He won't bend the rules for any of us, and while my desire might be a godly one to some extent, chances are that my real motive is for my receiving honor from people. All I know is, I am not able so far to write such a book, and I certainly know too little about God's glory. It is perhaps what happened when Moses walked up to the burning bush (to see why it didn't burn up) and God told him to stop. "Do not come any closer . . . take off your sandals . . . you are standing [on] holy ground" (Exod. 3:5). God does not explain everything we are curious about; instead He says, "Stop! Take off your shoes."

I know this much: The fear of God is what we must demonstrate in our hearts and by our lives as well as to respect His jealousy, and it is required of each of us. He wants all the glory for everything. Like it or not, that is the way He is. When He makes a covenant with His people He expects them to honor it. Israel didn't and they missed the very One they were so sure they would recognize and accept when He came. God rolled up His sleeves and inflicted blindness on Israel's best scholars and leaders. Relatively few Jews got in on the blessing.

Jonathan Edwards taught us that the task of every generation is to discover in which direction the Sovereign Redeemer is moving, then move in that direction. I can think of nothing worse than to miss seeing and participating in what God, in fact, instigates. If I am seeking His honor with all my heart I am assured I will not miss what He is doing in our day. When He is at work and people say, "That's not God," blindness in operation and almost certainly is traceable to fear of others and the pride in us that makes us want people's approval most of all. Yet He is a jealous God—always has been, always will be. Get used to it because that is the way He is; jealous.

There are therefore certain qualities among God's attributes, or characteristics, that are not regarded as very flattering when applied to people. Take, for example, the sensitivity of the Holy Spirit, which we have mentioned before. It is hardly possible to exaggerate how sensitive the Holy Spirit is, how easily He gets His feelings hurt. When Paul said, "Do not grieve the Holy Spirit of God, with whom you were sealed for the day of redemption" (Eph. 4:30), he used a word—*lupeite* (Greek translated "grieve")—that means "to get one's feelings hurt." When we speak of a person who is highly sensitive to criticism or who gets their feelings hurt easily, it is not a compliment. We say, "Be careful around that person, you have to walk on eggshells around them." It's not a nice thing to have said about you.

One of the most surprising aspects of God's personality, then, is that He is jealous by nature. Make no mistake, He is very up front about this trait. He even says that His very name is Jealous! "Do not worship any other god, for the LORD, whose name is Jealous, is a jealous God" (Exod. 34:14). Not a very flattering thing to have said about us. I don't want to admit when I am jealous because I don't want to appear vulnerable before you. But He admits it.

Jealousy is one of those traits about frail human beings that we can easily see in another person yet we are often the last to see in ourselves. We do not want to admit we have such insecurity. We dare not admit that a particular person gets our goat. It is embarrassing to admit the way we feel about a person, as often the real reason we do not like them is because we are jealous. We would not want that person we dislike to be so flattered!

Strange as it may seem, the jealousy that is seen as a product of our sinful nature (see Gal. 5:19–21) is the very word used to describe the God of the Bible. He can be like that and yet we can't! But is this unfair? I can only reply with the words God spoke through the prophet:

> "For my thoughts are not your thoughts, neither are your ways my ways," declares the LORD. "As the heavens are higher than the earth, so are my ways higher than your ways and my thoughts than your thoughts" (Isa. 55:8–9).

To put it plainly, when God does not get His way He becomes angry. He may not show it at first. Sometimes *the angrier He is the longer He waits* to bring vengeance. But when He does not have His way with us—His covenant people—His jealousy kicks in, and it is only a matter of time before it is openly manifested. He does not appear to be very nice when He does not get His way. It is this very thing that often, perhaps more than anything else, puts people off the God of the Bible. I will never forget how this struck me when I was at seminary in Louisville, Kentucky. While attending a preaching class, each of us had the task of preaching for twenty minutes to the other students. When my turn came I chose Romans 8:28 for my text: "And we know that all things work together for good to them that love God, to them who are the called according to his purpose" (KJV). I expounded it the way I continue to today—that whatever happens to us (good or bad or even our sin) will eventually work together for good if we love God and are "the called according to his purpose."

Many of my fellow students reacted very negatively. They replied that my sermon was "All God, God, God and all about His glory and nothing about us." Inwardly I was delighted my sermon came through like that—I could not have received a higher compliment. However, they hoped it would defeat me and humble me. But the episode was a kind of revelation to me; these students and I were operating on entirely different wavelengths. The very things they hated most about God, His glory and honor, specifically, were the very characteristics that thrilled me most.

One student, though no happier than the others, came to my defense somewhat and admitted, "After all, what R. T. has said about Romans 8:28 is what Paul really said—I just don't agree with Paul!" In other words, he didn't like the truth of Romans 8:28, which shows God's jealous love for His own, and how God is determined that whatever affects us affects Him as well and therefore He is determined to make sure all that happens to us, sooner or later, works together for good because His honor is at stake. It is a gracious fringe benefit of the truth of God's jealousy.

This is what happened when Ananias and Sapphira lied to the Holy Spirit (Acts 5:1–11). I doubt this couple was the first to lie to God, and neither would they be the last. But at that time God chose to show His jealousy and strike them dead, a clear manifestation of His glory. He was jealous for His glory in the Church. There was a very high level of His manifest presence in the Church in those days, and it was a foolish and dangerous thing to play fast and loose with His glory at such a time. I have long believed this is why Ananias and Sapphira did not get away with what they did at a time when God was doing wonderful things among His people. When God's power is being displayed, one would be better off playing with a million volts of electricity with wet hands than to play games with the Holy Spirit.

Consider what was going on in the book of Acts. A prayer meeting when the place was shaken—possibly by a small earthquake (Acts 4:31)—had resulted in great power and witness by the Holy Spirit to the people regarding Jesus' resurrection. So powerful was the Spirit's presence that the resurrection of Jesus was as real to them as if they had seen it with their own eyes. His power is so awesome that He can make clear the truths of redemption as though we were eyewitnesses. And when that kind of power is around we should take off our shoes and worship. A further result at that time was the people became utterly detached from material things. Some might say they lost their heads, and maybe they did, but for whatever reason, believers voluntarily sold their properties and laid the proceeds of the sales at the apostles' feet. As far as I know, we are not commanded to do this in any verse in the Bible, but it is what they chose to do.

Nobody was required to do what many were doing, including Ananias and Sapphira. Therefore Ananias and Sapphira could have opted out and said to the rest, "You can do this if you want, but we don't think we will." Had they, there would have been no problem. No, their fatal mistake was that they wanted to *appear* to be in on what was happening and pretended to lay all their proceeds at the apostles' feet, but in fact kept part of the money for themselves. And this action too might have been all right had they said, "We are only giving part of the money." But no. They pretended to give all as others had done. The high level of power and great measure of God's presence meant that the apostles discerned their mockery. God killed them.

I sometimes think of foolish things I have done in my lifetime—much worse (I would have thought) than what Ananias and Sapphira did. But God didn't kill me. He could have . . . perhaps He should have. And yet I think He would have, had there been a manifestation of His power and glory at the time.

The absence of that glory was possibly what saved me from being taken home abruptly to heaven like Ananias and Sapphira, as I do believe they were saved. Perhaps I should say I am glad that God was not in the process of showing His glory at times in my life which, if I make myself think about them, make me blush, and feel scared. Why should God be so gracious to me? Why should He not give me the treatment He gave to Ananias and Sapphira? I know only this: "The whole earth is full of his glory" (Isa. 6:3), which means that God could, if He wanted, call any of us at any moment to give an account of our thoughts and actions.

When Arthur Blessitt first came to Westminster Chapel in 1982, he shook us rigid. Upstanding and well-respected people were leaving the church. One deacon whom I loved said to me during the time of Arthur's visit, "The trouble is, do we really want revival?," candidly implying he wasn't so sure he wanted it after all. He could see the cost: overcoming pride, fear, tradition. True revival is so disruptive. Things were starting to happen in those days. It got messy. I always hoped for true and full-blown revival to come to Westminster Chapel while I was there. It never did, certainly not in the measure I longed for. I believe it will come. But had it come in the great measure I dreamed of, it might have meant a recurrence of people being found out and moved on like Ananias and Sapphira.

Have you ever wondered why certain people in Corinth were either weak, sick, or died because they abused the Lord's Supper? God's glory was at stake; his jealousy was aroused. The poor people of Corinth (slaves who had to work late) were being stepped on and walked over by the more affluent and smug believers who did not wait for the poor to arrive for communion. Paul had to tell them why some of them were weak or ill or dead. And yet those who were so disciplined by the Lord were truly converted, saved people. Paul said they were "judged by the Lord" in order that they not be condemned with the world, which would mean eternal punishment, not the chastening these had experienced (1 Cor. 11:17–34).

I have been guilty of some of the same things that characterized people who were severely judged by the Holy Spirit. I know I have been smug and arrogant and did not care one whit for the poor at earlier times in my life. I am so ashamed. What saved me was possibly the absence of the manifestation of the presence of God. I would hope I am in better shape now. But many don't want revival because smugness is one of the first things to be judged.

The revival that is needed (and which I happen to believe is coming) is the *Eschaton* (the Last Day) being brought forward to the here and now—at least for a while. It is when there is a clear sense of God, of joy and mourning, mercy and judgment, just as it will be when we all stand before the judgment seat of Christ (2 Cor. 5:10). On that day every deed will be exposed and then judged or rewarded. I therefore thank God, I am ashamed to say it, that revival did not come at certain times in my life when my heart was cold and full of doubt, cynicism, and unbelief. God was merciful to me, that's about all I can say. I would have to admit, moreover, that He was surely nice to me until I was brought to a place of repentance. Knowing as I do now something of the fear of the Lord, I have sought to live my life in a manner that, were God to show up, I would be ready. Being ready for revival is like being ready for the Second Coming. It comes suddenly.

"Between the times" is a phrase I learned from Richard Bewes to describe those seasons when God largely does not show His jealousy. He remains jealous while watching over us in whole detail. We should therefore live each day as if God would manifest His presence in great measure and such a time be great joy for us rather than grief.

For the Lord does not change (Mal. 3:6). His name is still Jealous. Were this truth to grip us as it should, it would literally change our thinking, our lives, and our attitude. God is jealous because He loves us so much, and it is truly wonderful that He is a jealous God. He wants only what is best for us. For this reason, His jealousy flares up when we show deference to other gods like the world, the flesh, and the devil. When we become more enamored with approval and honor from His people than the honor that comes only from Him, He doesn't like it one bit.

The purpose of this chapter and this book is to change the life of the person who reads it—you. When we see His displeasure and how He can show His anger, it ought to have at least a twofold effect: first, to thank Him for His patience with us and second, to be different from now on and live under the gracious fear of God.

It is an irony that the very thing God does to get our attention is often the very thing that puts us off Him: the hiding of His face, our unanswered prayers, or the way He chooses to be absent when we feel He is needed most. But this very thing is actually His way of leading us to repentance. The goodness of God leads us to repentance (Rom. 2:4 KJV), but that goodness appears at first to be the opposite of that, like striking people dead. Or manifesting His power in a manner that is utterly off-putting to us who are sophisticated.

I said above that I believe the revival that is needed is on the way. Get ready for it. It will be a mirroring of the true God and will show what really is in the hearts of men and women. In general, people will be unhappy with the God who will be manifested, at least at first. But many will be converted. It will be the manifestation of the God of the Bible for which most people are not prepared. Neither will it be our projection upon the backdrop of the universe. No human being could come up with the God who will shortly be revealed. But if that revival is for some reason delayed, you will still come face to face with him. For there is one inevitable fact: we are all going to die and "after that . . . face judgment" (Heb. 9:27). Therefore whether it is revival that is on the way or death, we will meet the true God.

We will certainly be out of our comfort zone then. But there is an exception to this. John talked about being "unashamed" before Him (1 John 2:28) and even having "confidence" on the day of judgment (1 John 4:17). What an amazing possibility—the consequence of walking in the light, that uncreated light of the true God in whom there is no darkness (1 John 1:5, 7). The result is the blood of Jesus cleanses us from all sin. That is how the amazing possibility of being bold before Him whether at his second coming, death, or during the revival I envisage is to come. It is seeing who the real God is and loving Him for being as He is. Will you love Him for being as He is?

What follows in the coming chapters is an attempt to describe Him little by little, like peeling the layers of an onion. But it is only an attempt. We will never see Him as he fully is until He unveils Himself in His ultimate glory at His Son's coming. And even then we will just begin to learn more about Him.

What If There Really Is a Hell?

I am not questioning whether there is a hell. But in the light of both massive repudiation of the historic teaching of eternal punishment by many stalwart scholars of the New Testament and also the strange neglect of preaching on this subject by those who claim they do believe in hell. I would define hell as

God's idea to create a place of unending conscious punishment of those who loved darkness rather than light and would not come to the light. Jesus said,

> This is the verdict: Light has come into the world, but men loved darkness instead of light because their deeds were evil. Everyone who does evil hates the light, and will not come into the light for fear that his deeds will be exposed. (John 3:19–20)

I think I have given more thought and prayer to this subject than any in this book or, for that matter, any in the Bible. The doctrine of eternal punishment of the lost does not seem right or fair to me, and I presume you feel similarly. If I could press a button and make one of two things happen to sidestep the matter, those two options would be:

1. The purported doctrine of annihilation (suffering which has an end in the soul being extinguished) is true after all; there is no eternal hell.
2. Universalism (everyone goes to heaven) is true—everybody will be saved and nobody lost.

I do not believe the Bible teaches either of these beliefs, but I would be glad if it did, or if it were discovered after we get to heaven that there was some loophole or clear teaching right before our eyes in Holy Scripture that we couldn't see before. There are people who think it is clear now and make a case for annihilation. Not many who call themselves Evangelicals would make a case for universalism; this has been the teaching of certain non-Evangelicals who do not hold to the infallibility of Holy Scripture as do I. Annihilation is the teaching that the lost will be utterly destroyed so that there are no remains of the person in any way—body, memory, soul, or spirit. Annihilation renders the lost as non-existent, as though they were never created in the first place.

You will recall my referring to Ludwig Feuerback at the beginning of this book. He claimed that God is nothing more than man's projection upon the universe. God does not exist, said Feuerbach; He exists only in our minds; we project a God who is "out there" who will look after us and take us to heaven when we die.

Given the premise, I ask: Whoever would have projected the doctrine of hell on the backdrop of the universe? What rational, normal, humane person would conceive of the teaching of hell? To me this is an appropriate question to put to the followers of Feuerbach. It disproves his theory—unless there is no hell—for no sensible human being would ever have come up with this teaching. This is not a God who only takes care of us or receives us in heaven but a God who is angry and punishes in a manner no person would have conceived or wanted to believe.

But could it be true? Is it conceivable that the New Testament really does teach us that people go to either heaven or hell when they die and that *both* places are inhabited by conscious people with memories and feelings and that both states never come to an end? Heaven is never-ending bliss occupied by those who received Jesus Christ as Lord and Savior; hell is never-ending punishment occupied by those who did not receive Jesus Christ as Lord and Savior.

Some of us might be tempted to say that the Bible was written by people in a pre-scientific age and that such a teaching was plausible and accepted then. But now that people have "come of age," to quote Dietrich Bonhoeffer (1906–1945), such a teaching is surely out of the question, not a few would say. Moreover, a loving God would not expect us to believe in such a horrible doctrine.

It has been somewhat surprising that good and capable scholars of the New Testament have come out of hiding in recent years to say they do not believe in conscious eternal punishment for the wicked, and to claim the Bible doesn't teach it either. There is some impressive evidence for their point of view, by the way. A lot of sincere Christians get indignant that such preachers exist ("How could they call themselves Christians?" some ask), but these ministers, it is only fair to say, do not reject eternal punishment merely because they don't want to believe it; they point to what they feel is the biblical evidence for the teaching of the annihilation of the wicked.

An entire book to treat the issue is called for; this section is but a drop in the bucket as to what is needed. I would recommend Wayne Grudem's *Systematic Theology.* I will mention briefly two points friends whom I love and respect want to say in support of the teaching of annihilation. The first is that the Greek word *apollumi* means "to perish" or "to destroy" and that Jesus said those who believe in him "shall not perish" (*apollumi*, John 3:16). Thus those who do not believe, then, simply perish: they are annihilated. I will respond to this shortly.

The second point those who teach annihilation make is that the traditional view of eternal punishment is largely based upon the Greek idea of the "immortality of the soul." Many of us have taken for granted that the soul of the person given to them by creation is immortal; the soul lives on even though the body dies. This is based partly on the fact that we are made in the image of God (Gen. 1:26–27). He alone has immortality in himself (1 Tim. 6:16), although he chose to bestow this on all the human race through creation. But we are now being told that this is only a Greek idea, not Hebraic, and that the Bible never taught the immortality of the soul in the first place. This makes it easier to accept the teaching of annihilation—a position taken by various cults over the years, including Jehovah's Witnesses, but which is now being embraced by a growing number of evangelicals.

According to this point of view, which is spreading like wildfire on both sides of the Atlantic, the soul is not given immortality until the person is born again. The traditional view (which happens to be my own) has been that the person is given immortality by creation—by being *born.* So if a person is given immortality of the soul when they are born, that person's soul survives death, but if the person is not given immortality of the soul until they are *born again,* only the *Christian*'s soul lives beyond the grave. The person who is not a Christian therefore does not have an immortal soul (according to this view); the person dies with no immortal soul to be annihilated. The person simply ceases to exist.

Some, however, teach that the unsaved will be raised to face judgment and will be annihilated after that. But the point is this: If the soul of the unsaved is not immortal, there is no hell awaiting the unregenerate; only the painless, instantaneous annihilation of the person by the fires of hell. These people want to emphasize that they do not deny hell; they deny only that hell is conscious, never-ending punishment. Hell to them means annihilation.

Regarding the Greek word *apollumi,* which is translated "perish" in John 3:16, there is no use of the word in the New Testament that clearly indicates annihilation. You can interpret it that way if you choose to in some places, but one would not likely think of annihilation if they were not looking for it and wanting to arrive at that meaning. If the New Testament writers wanted to make it clear that they meant annihilation they should have used the Greek word *ekmedenisis* (which clearly means "annihilation") or *ekmedenizo* ("to annihilate")—words that were in use then. Furthermore, there are times when *apollumi* (or the noun form, *apoleia*) could not mean "annihilation." For example, when some complained about the expensive perfume being poured on Jesus, they asked, "Why this waste?" (*apoleia*, the noun form of *apollumi*). "The perfume was wasted," they said. That is hardly annihilation. A modern equivalent is when an insurance company regards a wrecked car as a write-off. It is now waste.

Saying it with all love and honesty, this is what happens to the person who casts away the privilege that was theirs by not coming to the light; they will sadly be an everlasting waste. Forever. That is the meaning of the Greek word *apollumi* or *apoleia* when it is translated "destruction" or "perishing."

The question I often put to people who know neither Greek nor ancient philosophy is this: If you merely read the teachings of Jesus, without any bias whatsoever, what do you suppose *he* taught (even if you disagree with him)? And what do you really think his *hearers* perceived (even if they were ignorant and simple people)? Take the parable, or story, in Luke 16:19-31 as related by Jesus. Two people died—one of them, named Lazarus, went to Abraham's side, the other, who was called a "rich man" was found in hell. "In hell [Greek, *hades*], where he was in torment, he looked up and saw Abraham far away, with Lazarus by his side" (Luke 16:23). Since the physical bodies of Lazarus and the rich man were still in the grave, one assumes it was the souls, or spirits, of Lazarus and the rich man that are described. Whatever you want to call them, both men were very conscious after death; one was with Abraham (who apparently had been in that heavenly realm for hundreds of years), the other in torment.

You cannot make a parable stand on all four legs—meaning you cannot make a doctrine out of every point in a parable that is basically teaching one truth. But in this account, even if eternal punishment *isn't* the main point—I believe it is—Jesus would hardly have given throw away comments about a matter so awful if the truth about conscious punishment after death was not an assumption in His thinking or inconceivable by His hearers. If the account of the rich man and Lazarus was revealing new truth, what He said must be taken seriously. If this account only assumed these things, we need to see why they were mentioned.

As for the immortality of the soul being a gift of the Spirit at conversion and not creation, how does one explain the obviously unconverted rich man who was in conscious torment in *hades*—a term which means either a place of punishment or the grave? It wasn't his *physical body* that was suffering in hell, so it had to be his soul or spirit which survived the grave. What is obvious is this man was in conscious torment. Jesus also indicated that the two states are permanent and unchangable, both at Abraham's side—which I take to be a metaphor for Paradise or heaven—or in *hades*, which means "hell" in this parable.

The New Testament teaching on hell is based upon various descriptions which seem to be referring to the same thing: outer darkness, eternal punishment, weeping and gnashing of teeth, a furnace of fire, damnation, and other things. As to whether the fire is literal, I certainly hope it isn't and would make a case that it need not be literal. I would point to the real possibility that references to torment by fire are metaphors and not literal. For example, if Jesus could refer to eating His flesh and blood when He meant Holy Communion, or to raising up the temple in three days when He meant the resurrection of His body, or to the yeast of the Pharisees when He meant their teaching, then He could well have meant something other than literal fire when referring to hell. This is what I hope is true. It hopefully refers to the pain of the soul that is unbearable in the light of missing heaven and what could have been one's own eternal state. That scenario is horrible enough in any case.

I do not try to prove that hell exists in this chapter, just as Jesus did not try to prove that it existed—He only assumed it when He preached. He also taught that the only evidence for its existence is to be found in the Bible. The rich man in hell pleaded that Lazarus be raised from the dead in order to convince his lost brothers who did not believe hell existed. Jesus replied that they should believe the Word of God, the only basis for believing (Luke 16:30–31).

I believe hell exists. It was entirely God's idea. "Shall not the Judge of all the earth do right?" (Gen. 18:25 KJV). When John the Baptist warned people to "flee from the coming wrath" (Matt. 3:7)—arguably the first message of the New Testament, and eternal punishment was exactly what he meant—his warning made sense. I doubt people would *run* from coming wrath with much concern if they knew in advance it meant only annihilation. Annihilation becomes the same kind of non-existence the unbeliever is counting on when they die. What perhaps worries me most about the promotion of the idea of annihilation is that it hands on a silver platter a *theological* rationale to unbelievers, which is precisely what they were hoping was true in the first place. They say, "Why should I believe? Why should I give up my way of life? I will eventually end up as though I never lived, with no unending hell to fear."

The teaching of Jesus regarding hell was not meant to make us comfortable. He had more to say about hell than He did about heaven. People sometimes say, "I believe in heaven but I don't believe in hell." I say if there is no hell, there is no heaven. The two rise or fall together. Jesus' teaching on hell blasts us out of our comfort zone, because the God who conceived of the teaching of hell and who created hell is not very nice. It was not my idea, I can assure you. No human being would ever have thought this up.

But what if it is true? It makes all the difference in our outlook, our evangelism, our view of God, and our sense of gratitude that we ourselves will not spend eternity in hell. I think of William Booth's address to the first graduating class of the Salvation Army. He said he felt like apologizing to the graduates for keeping them for two years to learn how to lead a soul to Christ. "It would be better had you spent five minutes in hell," he said, because that way they would be effective soul winners on their own. But I thank God we don't have to spend any time there. Why? There are two ways by which God ultimately punishes sin: either by the sacrifice of His Son, whose blood *completely and eternally* satisfies His justice, or by the fires of hell, which never completely satisfy His justice, which is why hell is unending.

Is your God too nice? Is your God One who does not punish? Does He let you rest comfortably in your sphere of existence without any worries about the lost or the state of the Church being so irrelevant? Or the state of your own soul? Does He let you stay indefinitely in your comfort zone?

Not if He is the God of the Bible.

·4·

The "Yuck" Factor

> But God chose the foolish things of the world to shame the wise; God chose the weak things of the world to shame the strong. He chose the lowly things of this world and the despised things.
>
> 1 CORINTHIANS 1:27–28

I came to a conclusion years ago that God is on the lookout for what will make sophisticated people say "Yuck" when He is ready to show His glory again on the earth. Why? Paul tells us God's glory is always related to nullifying our fleshly wisdom in order to make room for what God calls wisdom, His glory. Indeed, Paul said that He chose the lowly and despised things in order that no one may boast or glory before the Lord (1 Cor. 1:29). All I know is, nearly every time God does something unusual it not only takes most people by surprise—whether it be the person He chooses or the manner in which He chooses to show up—but also makes the educated, cultured, and high-powered of this world say simply, "Yuck," an unsophisticated way of saying "Surely not." We often say or think it when we have a feeling of disgust, revulsion, or what is distasteful. Here is a passage that lies behind all that is to be said in this chapter:

> "For my thoughts are not your thoughts, neither are your ways my ways," declares the LORD. "As the heavens are higher than the earth, so are my ways higher than your ways and my thoughts than your thoughts." (Isa. 55:8–9)

The issue in this chapter is partly to answer those who say "That can't be God" when they come across an unusual or unprecedented manifestation that purports to be of divine origin or when a teaching springs forth that cuts across the way they had chosen to believe. Often our minds are made up and we don't want to be confused by any interpretation that threatens our comfort zone.

The thesis of this chapter is that God uses "yuck factors" to promote His glory. If something can make you say "Yuck," or "Surely not," be careful because God in heaven may just look down and say, "Good. This will work." Perhaps it emerges something like this: Behind the scenes there is a Trinitarian conference in the heavenlies where it is determined what will be the next thing that will cause smug people to say "Yuck." As Paul Cain frequently puts it, "God offends the mind to reveal the heart."

Why is this chapter important? First, God is a God of glory and will not cater to our sophistication. That which is highly esteemed, or highly valued, among men and women is an abomination in the sight of God (Luke 16:15). In other words, if religious people generally think something is worthy of being regarded as meriting the term "excellence," chances are that it makes God sick. He finds it detestable. Second, it is often the case that what religious people criticize most is the very thing God is in and the very thing of which He was the architect. Keep your ear to the ground and take note of the things with which religious people find fault. Once your list is compiled, check it carefully; do not be surprised if some of those very things that people are upset with are what God Himself initiated. What I call "when God plays hard to get" in this book comes into play. Let us also keep in mind what Jonathan Edwards taught us: That the task of every generation is to discover in which direction the Sovereign Redeemer is moving, then move in that direction. Edwards himself wrote about the surprising work of God in New England in his own day, and we pray for the equivalent or greater in our day. But be ready for things that you may find revolting. I'm sorry, but that is the way it is.

God has been doing this since the Fall of man in the Garden of Eden. In order to establish the forgiveness of sins through the sacrifice of blood, God first did it when He provided Adam and Eve with "garments of skin" to clothe them after their sin. They tried to cover their nakedness and shame by sewing fig leaves together but God instituted His carefully thought out plan for demanding substitution and satisfaction via the sacrifice of blood in order to appease His wrath and justice (Gen. 3:7, 21). The notion of salvation through atonement by the substitutionary death of another has probably been the most repulsive thing about the gospel of God. The popular Presbyterian minister Harry Emerson Fosdick (1878–1969) wrote that he certainly did not believe in this teaching, neither did he know any "intelligent" minister who did.

The Fall of Adam and Eve did not take God by surprise. Jesus was regarded in the New Testament as the lamb slain from the foundation of the world (1 Pet. 1:19–20; Rev. 13:8). Therefore the indication of his desire to forgive Adam and Eve was providing them with an atoning sacrifice for their sin in the Garden of Eden. Will we see Adam and Eve in heaven? Yes.

The scarlet thread of redemption continued in God's preference for Abel's offering over Cain's. Abel brought forth "fat portions from some of the firstborn of his flock" whereas Cain offered "fruits of the soil." God looked with favor on Abel but not with regard to Cain's offering (Gen. 4:3–5). This sent a signal early on that God will not respect the work of our own hands or what seems good to us—no matter how great our effort—but only that which he approves of; namely, the blood of a substitute. Charles Haddon Spurgeon used to say that there are two words that need to be in our theological vocabulary: "substitution" and "satisfaction." Substitution refers to one taking our place; satisfaction refers to the blood of the one who took our place which appeases God's justice. All sacrifices of blood in the Old Testament pointed to the ultimate sacrifice of the Lord Jesus Christ.

This still causes many learned and cultured people to say yuck. The idea of a need for blood sacrifice has been offensive from the time of Cain to this very moment as you hold this book in your hands. Today's sophisticated generation dismisses the idea of a God who demands a substitute for us or requires satisfaction by the shedding of blood. This notion goes back to a pre-scientific age, many say. Wrong. God always has looked for what will offend sophisticated people, possibly because He wants to put obstacles in our way to see if we will believe in His Word only. This is because faith—to be faith—is believing God without evidence for that belief. Only God's Word. "Faith is being sure of what we hope for and certain of what we do not see" (Heb. 11:1).

In other words, that which makes faith *faith* is when you keep trusting what God says although you are not able to prove your point. When people ask, "Why does God allow evil when He has the power to stop it?" I answer: To make room for faith. We wouldn't need faith if we could supply the answer to the problem of evil. Neither would we need faith if we could make ourselves look good before our accusers—whether they be sophisticated or not.

It isn't fun when respectable, intelligent people roll their eyes heavenward when they see our "foolish" stubbornness and adherence to God's chosen manifestation of His glory. The crowning blow among the hard sayings of Jesus came when He said, "Whoever eats my flesh and drinks my blood has eternal life" (John 6:54). Jesus made no attempt to explain Himself; He just let people vent their feelings—which they did. A very interesting and fruitful study is tracing the miracles of Jesus and noting how many times He waited for the Sabbath to arrive in order to offend the religious people of the day (see John 5:9; 9:14).

God's ultimate sacrifice was on Good Friday. We now know that the ancient sacrificial system under the Law pointed to the event of Jesus' crucifixion. But nobody knew it then, not when it was happening. It was God's secret weapon not only to take His people by surprise but also the devil. Satan conspired with Judas Iscariot, Herod, Pontius Pilate, the chief priests and leading Jews to crucify Jesus. But Paul says it was God's hidden wisdom from the beginning of time. "None of the rulers of this age understood it, for if they had, they would not have crucified the Lord of glory" (1 Cor. 2:8).

Indeed, had you walked into Jerusalem on Good Friday and asked the religious people, "What is God doing here today?" they would have answered, "It's Passover and we can hardly wait to celebrate it—if only that wicked thing on the cross outside the gate would hurry up and die." No one remotely dreamed at the time that God was in Christ reconciling the world to himself by the death of his Son (2 Cor. 5:19). Never forget that Jesus was crucified outside the city of Jerusalem and

God has continued to manifest His glory outside the camp. We therefore must be willing to go outside the camp—continually—and bear His reproach (Heb. 13:12–13). Some would even say, "The further out the better."

A funny thing happened to me when I preached at the Airport Christian Fellowship for John and Carol Arnott. It was an honor to be asked, it being the second anniversary of the so-called "Toronto blessing" (so named by the *Sunday Telegraph*). But when I got up to speak, using a text and sermon I knew backward and forward—"Let us then approach the throne of grace with confidence, so that we may receive mercy and find grace to help us in our time of need" (Heb. 4:16)—I could not preach it. I mean, I could not speak. I was literally kept from uttering two sentences intelligibly together. If you had paid me one million dollars tax free to preach my sermon on Hebrews 4:16 I could not have done it. After some fifteen minutes of intense and embarrassing struggle in trying to preach it, I felt an impulse that I should turn to Hebrews 13:13, not realizing what it said: "Let us, then, go to him outside the camp, bearing the disgrace he bore." I knew in a split second I was to give up trying to preach on Hebrews 4:16 and preach on Hebrews 13:13. Whereas up to then four thousand people were laughing their heads off, things got amazingly quiet. For the next twenty minutes I preached on that text with considerable liberty. Hundreds flocked to the front for prayer, including many ministers. It was an unforgettable night.

But my main point for bringing this up is that was the first sermon preached in the Toronto Christian Fellowship. Before then it was the Airport Vineyard Fellowship. The church had been sadly cut off and disenfranchised by the Vineyard hierarchy and on the very day I spoke it took its new name. They were thrust outside the camp. The sermon the Holy Spirit wanted was most appropriate. We must always be prepared to go outside the camp, even though it isn't fun. But it's good.

The yuck factor can now be defined. It is God's chosen stumbling block by which He intentionally puts off religious men and women. If He can come up with an event, activity, teaching, or manifestation by which "intelligent" and smug people will conclude, "This could not possibly be God at work," God says to Himself, "This will do nicely." "But we preach Christ crucified: a stumbling block to Jews and foolishness to Gentiles" (1 Cor. 1:23).

God's own people—His very elect—often initially underestimate the surprising time and way the Holy Spirit enters the scene. In a most insignificant and innocuous place, where he lay down to sleep, using a stone for a pillow, Jacob was made to admit, "Surely the LORD is in this place, and I was not aware of it" (Gen. 28:16). Speaking personally, almost every pivotal decision I had to make during my twenty-five years at Westminster Chapel was the outcome of having to overcome an initial negative reaction to what I encountered. It isn't fun to climb down—it is so embarrassing. But I had to do it more than once. I was never sorry.

Spirituality could be defined as closing the time gap between God's actual appearing and our acknowledgment of His presence. In other words, how long does it take for you to admit that that was God after all? It took years for some to concede it was God at work in New England between 1735 and 1750—now known as the Great Awakening. It took a good while before some people in Britain regarded the Welsh Revival as a genuine work of the Spirit and not emotionalism. I think of the British couple who sailed all the way from India to Southampton because they heard that true revival had broken out in Wales. But old friends—Christians—warned them that it was only Welsh emotionalism. The couple never went to Wales but returned to India. Sophisticated religious people have often stopped sincere Christians from embracing what is of God because it is so often tainted with what is undignified and not very traditional.

When Arthur Blessitt began witnessing on Sunset Strip in Hollywood, religious people said, "That can't be God." But it was. When he erected that large cross and hung it on a wall in what Arthur called His Place, people said, "That can't be God." But it was. When he claimed that the Lord told him to take the cross down from the wall and carry it on foot around the world, people said, "That can't be God." But it was. When I managed to get Arthur to speak at Westminster Chapel and stay for six weeks, religious people said, "That can't be God." But it was. The best decision I made in twenty-five years at the Chapel was to bring Arthur Blessitt to my old church.

So how long do you suppose it takes you to recognize God's presence? For some it takes years. For some it takes months. For some it takes moments. The degree to which we are familiar with God's own peculiar ways will likely determine how long we take to trace the rainbow through the rain.

When Charlie Colchester, the former churchwarden at Holy Trinity, Brompton, said to Lyndon Bowring and me in a Chinese restaurant in London's Soho, "Have you guys heard about this Toronto thing?"—referring to people falling on the floor and laughing—I wanted to say yuck. If you could have put me under a lie detector and asked whether I believed that what Charlie described that night was of God, I would have said no and passed with flying colors. For one thing, I didn't want it to be of God. I find that sort of thing offensive. Furthermore, I didn't want it to be of God because, if it really were, it would have come to Westminster Chapel first! *We* were the ones (I really thought this) who bore the heat of the day, witnessing in the streets of Victoria, praying for the manifestation of God's glory, and putting our reputation on the line. So if God were going to do anything in London it would have started with us!

I was wrong. For what was happening in those days at Holy Trinity, Brompton (called the "Toronto blessing"), as I later came to see, really was of God. It was hard to have to admit that. It wasn't easy to face my congregation, having previously publicly stated that it was not of God, and climb down. Some disagreed with me then and some still disagree. Some still continue to say yuck as I initially did.

Let me gently say that if your own reaction to what is happening in a church, even if it is strange and contrary to tradition, is to say yuck—or if you find yourself outside your comfort zone—please consider that there is a real possibility that God is behind the whole thing and that He takes responsibility for what you are uneasy with. You would not, would you, consciously want to be against what He is in? Since there is a pattern both in ancient Israel and in church history for God taking the blame for what was at first not appreciated, we must continually be open to the Lord and not be too hasty in dismissing what makes us feel uncomfortable.

As I will take pains to show below, not all that makes us think yuck is of the Holy Spirit—far from it. But it could be the Holy Spirit and a pattern in church history shows it often is Him at work.

I have, I hope, learned to be patient with people whose initial reaction is negative to the new and different (and strange). I've been there and continue to struggle with those whose style and emphasis is quite the opposite to my taste. I, therefore, do not want this book to be a recipe for how to be strange and please God. And I certainly don't want to be condemnatory. I only want you not to miss what God is up to and be deprived of blessing that you will be so thankful for later on. I am grateful to God for His patience with me and not taking me seriously when I have reacted negatively to what I later came to accept as being from Him.

In my book *In Pursuit of His Glory* I tell how I introduced our close friends Randy and Nancy Wall to the ministry of Rodney Howard-Browne. Rodney and Adonica Howard-Browne visited us in Key Largo and came to the Walls' home (where we were staying) for hamburgers. Rodney prayed for Randy who was immediately touched and overcome by the Spirit. Although he had no background to prepare him for what was coming (the church he attended did not even believe in the gifts of the Spirit), he began laughing uproariously for the next two hours. But his wife Nancy was not amused. "I am uncomfortable with this," she let us know.

It was not for another year or more that Nancy herself was blessed by the immediate and direct testimony of the Spirit. Her own manifestation of the Spirit was even more bizarre than laughing for hours. She was left with an urge to utter "Ho!" involuntarily—whether at home, church, or in a public restaurant. Yuck! Nancy was embarrassed by this at times, as we can understand. She is a cultured, sophisticated, and middle-class church member. This sort of thing had not been in her church background or upbringing, ever. So one day she asked me, "R. T., why does this urge to shout 'Ho!' come to me? Should I not repress it rather than embarrass myself and my friends?"

I replied, "Nancy, I think God does this to you to see whether you want the anointing of the Spirit more than anything else in the world. He has given you this stigma to see whether you are willing to bear it for the sake of His presence."

She immediately cried out, "Ho! Ho! Ho!"

We were outside and I was a little embarrassed. And then I said, "If you repress this, which you can do anytime you like, this will stop and probably never come back. And you will never forgive yourself and regret it as long as you live."

But Randy and Nancy began to feel uneasy in the church of which they had been pillars for over twenty years. I felt guilty, having introduced them to a dimension of the Spirit but also a stigma that, for some reason, came alongside at the same time. They eventually found another church where they are welcome. Though this has been an upheaval in their lives, they keep saying to me that they cannot thank me enough, that they would not go back to where they were for anything in the world.

If you ask, "R. T., do you ever 'Ho!' or do anything strange?" I answer, "Not yet." But the stigma for me has been different. It is more a case of having doors closed where I used to be accepted, noticing that old friends distance themselves from me, and hearing of things put in print that are unflattering and hurtful. But I too would not turn back for anything. I can state categorically that the increase of anointing more than compensates for any measure of loneliness or rejection. There is no substitute for the un-grieved presence of the Holy Spirit. It is just that He accompanies himself so often with an offence to test us whether He means more to us than the approval of friends. He is a jealous God.

I would have to admit that I have had more preparation than some when it comes to being open to the offensive ways of the Holy Spirit. My training for the position I have adopted as a way of life began many years ago. It certainly started when I was a child in my old church in Ashland, Kentucky. I can remember my mother literally running from one side of the church to the other during a service. I was six years old and embarrassed even then. I slipped outside the church. "What are you doing here, R. T.?" said one to me.

"I don't like the noise," I replied. After we got home I said to my mother, "Why did you do that?"

She replied, "Because I was so happy."

But I was hardly prepared for an advanced course in the surprising and unusual ways of the Spirit that came in the early months of 1956. My "Damascus Road" experience on 31 October 1955 had catapulted me into a new theological grasp of truth—the belief in election, predestination, and the eternal security of the believer. I came to this on my own—with no help from Nazarenes, the people of my old denomination. I thought I had a unique understanding of truth at first, that possibly nobody since the apostle Paul believed what I came to see just by reading the Bible and from what I sensed directly from the Holy Spirit. This continued until I found a group of Baptists in Ashland led by Pastor Henry Mahan, who accepted me and helped refine and clarify my "new" theology. It turned out that it wasn't new at all but rather historic Christianity. I am still amazed that God would do this for me. The "Damascus Road" experience was in fact my baptism in the Spirit. However, my theology is not what I want to talk about in this chapter.

A church service in which I was not present in my old church in Ashland, Kentucky, in April 1956 changed my entire life. It turned my world upside down. Dr. Billy Ball, to whom I will refer below, says it was the defining moment of his life as well. This service, perhaps more than any other (including those where I was present) did not shape my theology as such but it helped me to understand how the presence of the Holy Spirit in power can be anything but nice.

I was then a student at Trevecca Nazarene College in

Nashville, Tennessee, but also the pastor (traveling on weekends) of a small church in Palmer, about a two-hour drive from Nashville. What I shall describe was considered unusual, if not strange, even then when Nazarenes were less sophisticated. The pastor of the Ashland church had planned to hold nightly services but fell ill and asked his associate, Billy Ball, to conduct the meetings and do the preaching. My father wrote me a letter to tell me this but mainly to report how wonderful Brother Ball was preaching and said, "Son, he has been preaching with more power than I have witnessed since I was a boy." Dad wrote this to encourage me because he knew how much I enjoyed spending time with Billy Ball in those days. Billy had become my mentor in many ways.

My father's letter, however, did not greatly surprise me. The letter came two months after Billy himself told me what would happen in the Nazarene church in Ashland very soon. It was almost certainly my first exposure to the ministry of the prophetic. He told me in February 1956 that:

- the senior pastor would shortly become ill
- the pastor would ask Billy to do the preaching
- Billy would be given unusual power
- something would happen that would thrust Billy right out of this church

I remember when he told me this, at his home in Ashland, and how a most unusual but sweet presence of the Holy Spirit fell in the room. It was as though there was a glow in the center of the room. I also remember believing in my heart that I would one day be in an international ministry but could not imagine how that would happen. Nazarenes were very provincial and I saw myself then as a Nazarene forever—no matter what. Therefore I wondered how I could be involved in a world-wide ministry.

What happened was this. The pastor announced that he would preach in a series of nightly meetings in April 1956. A worship leader, known then as a song evangelist, was brought in to lead the singing. But a few days before the meeting was to begin, Billy received a phone call to see the pastor. I remember Billy saying to me, "The only thing that troubles me is that in my vision the pastor was in bed in a room that I did not recognize but neither was it a hospital room, so I don't know how this will happen." But when he arrived at the parsonage in answer to the pastor's wife's phone call she directed him upstairs and said, "Oh, he is in the room to the right as you come to the top of the stairs, not our regular bedroom." When Billy entered the room, it was exactly as he had seen it in a vision.

The pastor asked Billy to preach in the services. Billy did so and preached night after night with unusual power. That is when my father wrote the letter to me. The thrust of Billy's preaching for four nights was based largely on two verses:

> How can ye believe, which receive honour one of another, and seek not the honour that cometh from God only? (John 5:44 KJV)

> And he said unto them, Ye are they which justify yourselves before men; but God knoweth your hearts: for that which is highly esteemed among men is abomination in the sight of God. (Luke 16:15 KJV)

But the pastor showed up on the Thursday evening and said he would preach from now on. This decision would have pleased everybody since the pastor was regarded as one of the greatest preachers of the denomination, but people noticed a difference in the atmosphere. The pastor, though greatly loved and respected by all the people, did not seem to have his usual power in preaching, certainly nothing like what the growing congregations had witnessed when Billy did the preaching that week.

Three men, all members of the church—Ed, Jack and Howard—approached Billy to see if he would join them for a time of prayer. The four men began to pray on that same Thursday evening after people went home from church. They ended up praying for almost the entire night. I later talked with some of these men and asked them what it was like. I wanted to know because the fallout of this prayer meeting would have a major effect on my own life. Two of them said they felt a burden for one man in particular but did not discuss it with each other; it turned out to be the same person each felt led to pray for. One of the men told me he had a vision of hell—or what he assumed must be hell. He said he saw only faces, or heads, of people floating in what looked like burning sulphur. Their faces were contorted and in despair. He recognized them as people he knew and was shocked since they were regarded as strong members of the church. The four men did not talk with each other during the night but prayed until about five o'clock in the morning. They returned to their homes in order to go to work that day. Billy assumed he would not be asked to preach on Friday evening since the pastor had returned to the pulpit the evening before. But he was asked during the day to conduct the Friday evening service and preach.

The four men met at church at seven o'clock on Friday evening to spend more time in prayer. The service began at 7:30 with congregational singing. Billy left the three men in the room in which they were praying and took his seat on the platform. During the congregational singing the three other men burst into the service and began to exhort the people. Two of the men took their seats after a few minutes, but Ed kept it up—walking up and down the center aisle of the church "like a wild man," according to my dad. The singing came to a halt while Ed addressed the shocked congregation. The organist, who happened to be my Aunt Ruth, began to play with the hope that Ed would take the hint and sit down, but he didn't. He even told Aunt Ruth to stop playing. She did. Ed continued to speak to the people, shouting with all his might. My dad, who witnessed the whole episode, bowed his head and prayed that Ed would please stop this ranting and raving.

But he didn't. As for my father, he was quite out of his comfort zone. Ed continued, urging the people to repent. He then began to say that someone present was seriously grieving the Holy Spirit, that this person was holding back what could be great revival. Different ones present later told me they thought it could be them—as if to say in their hearts, "Is it I?" Ed kept exhorting the congregation of about 400 for nearly thirty minutes and then stated that *Ichabod* was written over the door of the church. The Holy Spirit was being quenched. The pastor, who had asked Billy to take the service, unexpectedly turned up and took his seat on the platform. Ed did not see him but continued, "I see a coffin, the person in it is holding up the revival. I know this man. I love this man. I love him very much. I know his address. I fear for this man."

My dad continued to plead with the Lord that this would end. Whereas some sensed great fear and personal conviction, my father and grandmother, who was also present, only wanted Ed to stop his unreasonable, rather irrational behavior. At some point during Ed's shouting to the people a haze settled on the service. Not all saw it. My dad didn't see it. Ed saw it but thought that something had gone wrong with his eyes since he could not see past the haze. He kept rubbing his eyes to see better and had no idea what it was or what it meant.

The song evangelist decided to stand in the pulpit and ask the people to sing a well-known song called "The Unclouded Day." At this point Billy walked to the pulpit and motioned for the song leader not to proceed since Billy wanted to say something. My dad was greatly relieved to see Billy take charge because it was assumed Billy would bring a sense of sanity and order to the service that had become completely out of control. The service was almost like a nightmare to some. But all were pleased that Billy would take over.

"This is the greatest demonstration of the Holy Ghost I have ever seen," Billy said. My dad said to himself, "Oh no, Brother Ball is condoning this wild fanaticism." But Billy began reading aloud the account of Ananias who lied to the Holy Spirit. He read the first five verses of Acts 5 and sat down. A number of people got out of their seats and came to the altar. Six or seven were reportedly converted or, at least, got spiritual help. At this point the pastor took charge and asked if anybody else wanted to come forward for prayer, then dismissed the service.

There were mixed reactions to the service, which turned out to be historic in many ways. Some felt a great conviction of sin and feared they were the person Ed had in mind. From all accounts it was no time for laughter but a great sense of fear and sobriety. One old lady, highly respected for her godliness, said, "I thought the days of Holy Ghost manifestations like this were over but this is the best I have seen." Others, however, were horrified and upset that such an undignified service was allowed to continue. No one thought it was very nice.

On the Saturday evening the pastor was feeling better and

did the preaching. After the service he asked to meet with the four men—Howard, Ed, Jack, and Billy Ball—and said to them, "Who are you men after?" They were taken aback by the question and did not know how to answer. They all said, "We are not after anybody." Then the pastor focused on Ed, "Who are you after?" Ed replied he was after no one but admitted that he had a burden to pray for him, that is, the pastor who was questioning them. The pastor then asked Ed, "Who did you have in mind last night when you exhorted the people like you did?" He replied that it was the pastor himself he had in mind on the Friday night.

The pastor then turned to each of them to see if they agreed with Ed, asking Billy first. Billy said that he had a burden to pray for the pastor during the all-night prayer meeting that began Thursday evening but had not said this to a single soul. Each man then said that they felt in their hearts that Ed had the pastor in mind during the Friday service but none of them discussed this among themselves. This very moment, then, when the pastor called the four men for this meeting, was the first time they actually spoke to each other on the subject.

At this point the pastor asked them, "What have I done? What sin have I committed?" No one knew what to say in reply. The pastor then knelt at the altar—they thought he did so mockingly—and said, "I am the penitent, now you men pray for me." The men felt helpless and were not able to pray at all. They did not believe the pastor was really sincere. They did their best to pray but felt no liberty in doing so. After an hour or so they all dispersed and went to their homes.

The next morning, Sunday, the pastor phoned each of the members of his board. My dad was on the board and told me verbatim what happened. "I now know who the men had in mind Friday night," he said to my father.

"Who?" my father anxiously asked.

"Me."

"No, it can't be you, surely not."

"Yes, I am the man."

My father was disgusted with the four men, including Billy Ball. How dare they question the pastor, Dad thought. This pastor was regarded as one of the greatest preachers of the denomination and also very humble and godly.

Within forty-eight hours Billy Ball was dismissed as the associate pastor of the Nazarene church and immediately had to find a place to live and get any kind of job he could find. It will be recalled that I was not present at this service. But I received a letter from my father a few days later. Whereas the previous letter from my father sang Billy Ball's praises, this letter said: "Son, have nothing to do with Billy Ball. Do not write him, do not call him. Something terrible has happened in our church. Billy Ball has been asked to leave and resign as associate pastor. Nothing immoral. But have nothing to do with him."

I was puzzled. Sobered. As I drove in my car after reading the letter I had a clear witness of the Holy Spirit—as clear as an audible voice—to turn to Philippians 1:12, not knowing what it would say. Nothing like this had happened to me before. I stopped the car, opened my Bible to read it: "But I would ye should understand, brethren, that the things which happened unto me have fallen out rather unto the furtherance of the gospel" (KJV).

I knew at once that it referred to Billy Ball. To me it meant that Billy had not done anything wrong, whatever had happened, had been led by the Holy Spirit. But it would equally refer to me, as I would see later. For that verse held me more than anything else over the next several years. All this led to the first break with my dad, the most godly and sincere Christian I have ever known. It was the beginning of a long, hard, bleak era in which I would crave vindication more than the world itself.

This then is why the aforementioned service, though I was not present at it, changed my life. Nothing was ever to be the same again. One year before I was given a brand new 1955 Chevrolet by my godly grandmother. She was widely regarded as possibly the most saintly elderly woman in that church. As I said above, she was also present in that extraordinary service. But my standing on the side of Billy Ball, combined with a new theological perspective, changed everything. She took the car back. I would ask myself in those days, How could she do this? Had I broken with God? Had I gone out into the world? Had I fallen into sin? No. But I broke with her concept of God. It led to her disinheriting me. My dad went through deep grief, even comparing it to what he felt when my mother died three years before.

Who was right? Was the pastor right to phone the key members of the church the Sunday morning after confronting the men? Was the church board right to dismiss Billy Ball? Or do it so soon? Was Billy Ball right to walk to the pulpit, endorse all that had happened, and then read Acts 5:1-5? Was Ed right to interrupt the service as he did—and then cry out that God had written *Ichabod* over this church? Was my dad right to order me to break all connections with Billy Ball? Was my grandmother right to take back the car and eventually disinherit me? And was I right to stand with Billy Ball and take the view that the service—strange and terrible as it seemed to be—was actually orchestrated by the Holy Spirit? Would God really be in this? If so, how could such godly people miss it?

I return to the matter of the haze. During the Friday service when a haze filled the auditorium, Billy Ball saw it. He has commented to me many times that he never knew such power in all his life as he had in the pulpit as he read from Acts 5:1–5, that it is even difficult to imagine any ancient prophet having more power than he felt as he read those verses. As for Ed, he certainly saw the haze but was confused by it and was afraid to mention it to anybody for weeks lest they say even more critical things to him.

The haze was the *kabodh* (Hebrew), meaning the *shekinah*, glory of God. It is what disrupted the priests in their work in the temple. "Then the temple of the LORD was filled with a cloud, and the priests could not perform their service because of the cloud, for the glory of the LORD filled the temple of God" (2 Chron. 5:13–14; cf. 1 Kings 8:10–11). Jack Hayford described this phenomenon in his own testimony, which I heard him give. When he had a small church of about 300 people, he walked into his auditorium one Saturday (with nobody else in it) and saw this haze. "It's what you think it is," the Lord said to Jack. Then the Lord said to him, "I will give my glory to dwell in this church." From that very time his church began to be blessed in ever-increasing measure and became the wonderful church it is today.

But the *kabodh* in that Kentucky church service was not a promise of growth and blessing. Quite the opposite. It was instead a seal of the Holy Spirit on that unforgettable service in which people thought such happenings could not possibly be instigated by God. God is surely too nice to do that sort of thing. Although there was a mixed reaction, most concluded that it was not of God. But I believe that it was.

My old church in Ashland continued for years as if nothing happened. To me it was not unlike the temple in Jerusalem continuing after Jesus' death on the cross. Though the veil inside the temple was torn from top to bottom, the priests went back to business as usual. There was no outward sign or even hint that God wrote "Ichabod" over the temple. In much the same way, those who continued to worship at the Ashland church, as far as I know, sensed nothing different. It is like that statement of the Episcopal rector who said, "If the Holy Spirit were completely withdrawn from the Church today, ninety percent of the work of the Church would continue as if nothing had happened." But from that time, slowly but surely, the spirit and power of my old home Nazarene church went down, down, down. Within a generation it had lost its strategic influence and the numbers dwindled to the size of a small church. As for the pastor, he soon lost the support of many who had defended him at the time—even those who were most indignant against Billy and the three other men. He continued until, a few years later, he died a premature death.

Many people of the Ashland congregation warned me that I would not be used of God for taking this stand. Billy and I would "eat dust," a number of them said. My father sincerely believed I moved right out of God's will and was bringing judgment on myself, and with tears he continually and lovingly but firmly warned me. By siding with Billy Ball and suggesting that the existing pastor could have seriously quenched and grieved the Holy Spirit, my dad said we had gone against God's anointed and we would pay dearly. In addition to all the above, my own radical theological change paralleled all this; I came to embrace the doctrines of sovereign grace and this confirmed all the more (certainly to my dad) that I was utterly in the wrong.

I tried not to let that bother me too much, but it still hurt to be looked upon with disdain. I went through times when I wondered if I had it wrong after all. At times I even hoped I was wrong, especially after coming to Westminster Chapel. It was easier to dismiss the aforementioned episode as utter fanaticism so I need not fear God would do anything strange in the Chapel, or require me to have to tolerate such strangeness. The person to give me the most objectivity about that service in 1956 came many years later from none other than Martyn Lloyd-Jones. On two different occasions, over three years, I repeated the story, hoping he would look at me and say (as he had done dozens of times on other issues), "Now look here. This was quite wrong." Or something like that. But no. Both times he came up with the same thing: God was indeed wanting to do something in that church and the men were led of the Holy Spirit. Dr. Lloyd-Jones frequently surprised people by his ability to recognize God at work when no one else could.

In the summer of 1979, some twenty-three years later, my beloved dad visited us in London, approximately two years after I became the minister of Westminster Chapel. I was not prepared for what he unexpectedly said to me. Given my own dad's culture and background I found this quite extraordinary. I heard him utter words for which I used to long. I could hardly believe what I was hearing, but he actually said to me: "I'm sorry, son, I was wrong. God's hand has been on you all these years and I am so proud to have you as a son." As for Billy Ball, he felt forced to leave his old denomination in 1956 but went from strength to strength in another church. Though Billy and I were not destined to have a ministry together (as I used to suppose), he became the pastor of a church that grew to be the largest church in the state of Ohio. He became one of the most popular and respected preachers in his movement and has been honored by many thousands from all over the world for his faithfulness to God and the Word.

The question is: Are there objective tests by which a person who doesn't want to be deceived and who doesn't want to miss out on God's blessing can be guided? I really do wish I knew the answer to this. I have my own dilemma in this area. For why is it that sincere Christians who are devoted to pleasing God, like my own father, can miss the mark regarding God's will and presence? How could my dad or my godly grandmother be on the wrong side of the issue in those hard days of 1956? Why did not everybody see the haze? Or would they have recognized it for what it was? What were the ingredients in the Ashland service that led Dr. Martyn Lloyd-Jones to believe it was of God?

I cannot be sure how I would have reacted had I been present. Had not the Holy Spirit given me Philippians 1:12 at a critical time I might well have sided with the majority who felt that Billy Ball and Ed were deceived and governed solely by the flesh. I would never have been friendly with Billy Ball again, neither would I have had him as a mentor.

I had opposed the Toronto blessing until I watched a close friend fall on his face when prayed for in my old vestry. He was not by nature open to that sort of thing and had not even heard of the Toronto phenomenon but politely allowed a ministerial friend to pray for him. When he went to the floor involuntarily and lay there helplessly for ten minutes, I began to fear I was on the wrong side of that issue. *I cannot think of anything worse than being near where God is at work but missing out on it because of my own prejudice.*

At the end of the day—as to who immediately recognizes the Holy Spirit and who doesn't—I think it comes down to the sovereignty of God. There is more than one sphere in which the sovereignty of God works. He is sovereign in salvation; He saves some but (apparently) not all. He is sovereign in healing; He heals some but (apparently) not all. The gifts of the Spirit are meted out as He sovereignly determines (1 Cor. 12:11, 18). So too, I must conclude, with the unusual ways God is pleased to show up. He opens the eyes of some and lets the rest say yuck. But sometimes, thankfully and mercifully, He changes those of us who say yuck first and graciously humbles us.

All I know is, we must try not to be hasty in rejecting what isn't very appealing. We may have to eat our words. His ways are higher than our ways. He has chosen the foolish things of the world to confound the wise. As Jesus put it, "I praise you, Father, Lord of heaven and earth, because you have hidden these things from the wise and learned, and revealed them to little children. Yes, Father, for this was your good pleasure" (Matt. 11:25–26). A further irony—call it God's sense of humor if you like—is that so many who are proponents of the sovereignty of God (and sometimes think they have a franchise on this truth) are sovereignly blinded to the things of the Holy Spirit. I wish it weren't so. They remind me of A. W. Tozer's words, that there is nothing worse than people who don't have the Spirit but who talk a lot about the Spirit as though they did.

Let us pray that God will somehow keep us from grieving His Holy Spirit and graciously let us in on what He is up to. Let us be patient with those who oppose what we accept; for were it not for the grace of God we too would be where they are. I just pray that God won't be so nice to you and me as to leave us in our smugness and pass us by when it comes to knowing His ways.

No, it isn't the greatest fun in the world to be found outside your comfort zone or to bear any kind of stigma. But down the road the reward is worth the wait.

· 5 ·

THE SIN JESUS HATED MOST

> The Pharisee stood up and prayed about himself: "God, I thank you that I am not like other men."
>
> LUKE 18:11

I had an experience in Jerusalem recently for which I was not prepared. Some of us, including the former Archbishop of Canterbury and his wife, Lord and Lady Carey and Canon Andrew White of Coventry Cathedral, had a Sabbath meal on a Friday evening with a prominent Israeli rabbi and his family. It was a wonderful evening. Rabbi David Rosen, the Jerusalem-based International Director of Interreligious Affairs of the American Jewish Comittee, endeared himself to all of us as he demonstrated with his wife and two children what their Sabbath evenings are like. It even brought us to tears. If most people we may be tempted to call Pharisees are cold, I have to admit that this man, a modern self-confessed Pharisee, was very warm.

But what startled me prior to my getting to know him—as well as discussing the matter with him—was the complimentary way he had referred to a Pharisee. I was stunned at first because nearly all I have known about a Pharisee is not good, and calling one a Pharisee therefore is not a compliment, to put it mildly. But Rabbi Rosen wants to be seen as a Pharisee in our day and wears the label as a badge of honor. To make sure I wasn't misunderstanding him I asked him if indeed I rightly discerned this? Absolutely, he replied. He has since sent an informative email on the matter.

You might like to know that he has read this chapter and the one which follows. However, he sees a very important distinction between those Pharisees Jesus is recorded as addressing and Pharisees as they are truly to be understood. He also believes that today's successors in Israel, of which he is one, bear no resemblance to those described in the New Testament. Not only that, he told me that he would feel much the same as I do toward those Pharisees Jesus is recorded as addressing. Rabbi Rosen and I are in continuing dialogue about this. We may even write a book together on it one day.

In the four Gospels, the Pharisees are portrayed almost entirely as the bad guys. And yet I keep in mind that on at least one occasion Jesus accepted an invitation to have dinner with a Pharisee (Luke 11:37). The meal was paralleled by Jesus ruthlessly exposing the hearts of the Pharisees—whom he tended to put altogether in one lump—and called them "You foolish people" (v. 40). The Pharisee might have been a nice man, but Jesus was not very nice to him.

The Pharisees (a word which probably means the "separated ones") emerged in the second century BC. They were a strict sect made up mostly of ordinary Jews, unlike the Sadducees who were members of the families of priests. Pharisees were far more numerous than Sadducees but not so prestigious. The Pharisees kept closely to the Mosaic Law and often embellished the Law with countless rules so that these rules were very hard to keep. They saw themselves as a cut above everybody else. They counted work on the Sabbath as walking more than a kilometer from one's town, carrying any kind of load, or lighting a fire in the home. It led to people being concerned to keep the Law in every detail. The Pharisees believed that their rules built a fence around the Law so that by keeping these rules people would be in less danger of disobeying the actual Law of God.

One must not forget that many of them were no doubt pious men. Some scholars reckon that when Jesus described the Pharisee in the parable in Luke 18:9–14, some Pharisees really did do such things as He boasted of—fasting twice a week and giving a tenth of all they earn, not to mention the fact that they would never be guilty of wrongdoing such as robbing or committing adultery. They were regarded as the truly righteous people of their day. They were without question the backbone of their synagogues and would in some cases be like certain Evangelicals today who carry their big black Bibles to church and would never smoke or touch a drop of alcohol or watch a movie that was anything but for the whole family. But they tended to look down on those who did not keep their rules and called such people sinners. Remember too that Nicodemus, who was a secret follower of Jesus, was a Pharisee. So was the apostle Paul before he was converted.

Dr. Martyn Lloyd-Jones used to relish telling the story (which I have in print elsewhere but which is too good not to mention here) of two unforgettable weeks he and Mrs. Lloyd-Jones spent in America many years ago. The first week was with a very religious couple in White Sulphur Springs, West Virginia, who were the quintessence of American fundamentalism. This man and his wife were disgusted with "so-called" Christians who smoke and drink. According to Dr. Lloyd-Jones, it seemed his host could never get through a meal in the entire first week without referring in disdain to "these people who call themselves Christians" who smoke or use alcohol. For one thing, he said, it is "blowing away money," wasting God's provision. Dr. Lloyd-Jones looked across the table and asked the lady, who dressed very fashionably, how much her dress cost. Things got very quiet as it was ridiculously expensive. When the week was over, even though they enjoyed much of it, the Lloyd-Joneses were rather relieved to get away from them.

But there is more. Their next stop was in Grand Rapids, Michigan, where they were to spend a week. They were amused to note that the man who picked them up at the airport was smoking a big cigar, and when they got to his house he said, "Doctor, would you like a whiskey?" Both Dr. and Mrs. Lloyd-Jones were intrigued at the contrast between the two couples. Yet Dr. Lloyd-Jones stressed that both couples, though very different, equally loved the Lord.

But that is not the end of the story. On the Sunday night after the church service in which Dr. Lloyd-Jones preached, he noticed a Howard Johnson® restaurant and said, "Oh look, there is a Howard Johnson's. I love their ice cream. Do you suppose we could stop and have some?" Things went quiet, but the host politely pulled over and went into the parking lot. As they sat at the table Dr. Lloyd-Jones noticed that all were quiet. He spoke up, "Is anything wrong?"

"No, of course not," the man replied.

"Now look here," said Dr. Lloyd-Jones, "We have been together for a few days and something is clearly wrong. Please tell me what it is."

The man finally agreed. "The problem is today is the Sabbath and we do not buy anything on the Sabbath."

When they returned to their room, Dr. Lloyd-Jones said to his wife, "It seems everybody has to have something they are against so they can feel a bit righteous. I wonder what it is with us? There must be something!"

Whatever the case, this is true with so many of us; it seems there are one or two areas, at least, in which we have strong views about something. These views may unconsciously make us think they compensate for other liberties we allow for ourselves (if not too many know about them!). An Episcopalian joke in America is: What is the difference between Southern Baptists and Episcopalians? Answer: The Episcopalians speak to each other in the wine store. I have seen it a thousand times, the best of people who have their secret sins—even if they are not really sins but controversial practices they allow. Equally they have one or two strong views about this or that which gives them a feeling they haven't gone completely off the deep end.

It is said that when the German Christians saw the American believers with all their gold and diamonds they were so shocked they dropped their cigars into their beer! I am also reminded of the story of when the great Charles Spurgeon, who loved a cigar, met the famous D. L. Moody. Moody rebuked Spurgeon for smoking. Spurgeon replied that there was not one word in the Bible about "this," referring to his cigar, but that there was a lot in the Bible about "that," gently poking Moody's extended stomach. Let no one think I am happy about cigars.

As for "rules," I am often asked by my British friends "why do preachers in America never seem to say a word against being fat and overweight?" This was always an awkward question put to me, especially knowing that I had many precious friends who were obviously overweight. Moreover, these are people who sincerely love the Lord. This kind of question would come up nearly every time we would have an American choir come to Westminster Chapel to sing. I was always sadly conscious, seeing huge, overweight people make their way to the galleries on each side of the pipe organ to sing for us. As I listened—and watched—I knew exactly what my people were thinking. I did indeed wonder if pastors in the United States ever touched on the matter of our bodies being temples of the Holy Spirit when it comes to food. So, after our retirement in America, imagine my amazement when I slipped into a church one Sunday morning to hear a sermon entitled "Fat Christians." I thought, "Oh good. What courage this pastor has. I never thought I would see the day a minister would address this matter." But the sermon was rebuking Christians who were fat in Bible knowledge and never witnessed to the lost.

Living in America again, I do sympathize with people who are overweight. They do not want to be this way. And yet I think of the way food is pushed at us right, left, and center. How there is hidden sugar that is put in cereal, ketchup, and many other things; hidden fats in so much food—not to mention the inexpensive restaurants that often include "all you can eat" buffets. Christians by and large do not smoke or drink in America but they too often compensate with food.

These lines may put some readers out of their comfort zone. I don't mean to be unfair. But I would say lovingly that our bodies are the temples of the Holy Spirit (1 Cor. 6:19–20; 2 Cor. 6:16). It is now well known that smoking causes cancer. But according to the Harvard School of Public Health, the number of cancer cases a year in the United States that can be attributed to obesity is staggering: breast cancer—11 percent; colon cancer—15 percent; endometrial cancer—49 percent; esophageal cancer—39 percent; kidney cancer—30 percent; non-Hodgkin's lymphoma—20 percent; pancreatic cancer—14 percent. This is to say nothing of diabetes, heart problems, high blood pressure, kidney disease, and a multitude of other ailments. As for witnessing to the lost, our appearance can speak more loudly than words, and I often wonder what non-Christians must think about us who lack self-discipline in our private lives. However, the problem is that issues such as smoking and drinking become like the Pharisees' rules, which you had to keep or be looked down on.

Given the fact that Pharisees were pious, faithful, and the stalwarts of the synagogues in ancient Judaism, why was Jesus so hard on them? Should he not have congratulated them, as if to say, "You are greatly needed here in Jerusalem these days. I can't imagine what things would be like were it not for you." No. He never congratulated them once or gave the slightest hint they were either needed or appreciated. He was harsh and rugged with them. Why? The answer to this question, which will come clearer as we proceed, is why the present chapter is so important to this book.

What is most interesting to me is that Jesus was patient, loving, and gracious to the woman caught in the sin of adultery, unlike the Pharisees who were delighted and supposedly indignant that they found this woman in the act of sin (John 8:1–11). Jesus never appeared to show tender feelings toward the Pharisees. He was not nice to them, despite the fact that they upheld the infallibility of the Bible, believed in resurrected life beyond the grave (unlike the Sadducees), and adhered to a number of practices which Jesus also affirmed.

When I was a young Christian I used to wonder why so much attention was given in the four Gospels to the Pharisees since they do not exist today. Was this not a waste of space? Why should we have to read about irrelevant people? I have since learned of course that Pharisees do indeed exist today. And I fear I am one of them in too many ways. But other reasons we must listen to what Jesus said to them and about them include:

- His words were infallible
- His judgment perfectly mirrored the will of the Father (John 5:19)
- we too would be the objects of Jesus' firm words to the degree we also are Pharisees

We are not exempt. His ruthless exposure of the ways of the Pharisees bears our attention. If Jesus was angry with them then, the Father feels the same way about us now.

What Jesus therefore said to the Pharisees—and about them—must be taken seriously and applied to our lives today. I for one do not want to be a Pharisee. Do you think there is a possibility you could be a Pharisee? To the degree I am one I should be most uncomfortable. If Jesus was not nice to the ancient Pharisees I should be very worried indeed if He is nice to me when I am very like them.

The Pharisees' Comfort Zone

Their Traditions

Their extra-biblical rules became a tradition that you were required to keep or you did not love God or respect the Law. Some Pharisees came up to Galilee all the way from Jerusalem just to ask Jesus, "Why do your disciples break the tradition of the elders? They don't wash their hands before they eat!"(Matt. 15:1–2). Imagine being so threatened by Jesus that one walks for three days just to see why He did not keep certain rules. This washing of hands was not merely a health matter, by the way, it was a ritualistic action that showed you adhered to the "party line."

Is tradition important to you? Tradition was very important to the Pharisees. This doesn't make you a Pharisee. There is nothing particularly wrong with tradition. Sometimes it is quite valuable. The problem is, we end up equating it with the Word of God and, if we are not careful, find it difficult to separate the two—thus making tradition idolatrous.

Some good people do this with the Schofield Bible. This popular Bible has notes that accompany the Word of God which have unwittingly led many Christians, perhaps more so in America, not to know the difference between Schofield's own comments (some of which are good) and the unedited Word (which alone is infallible). I have had people heatedly quote "Scripture" to me from a Schofield Bible, only to discover they were reading what Schofield said in the margins or at the bottom of each page. My point is this: When Scripture and commentaries on Scripture are put alongside each other with equal authority so that one is revered as much as the other, it is idolatry. That is what the Pharisees did with their rules which turned into traditions which turned into Law.

I used to say England is the most traditional country in the world and Westminster Chapel was the most traditional church in England. Sandy Millar lovingly said to me that we were "back in the '60s," meaning that our style resonates with the way churches were in the 1960s. I took him seriously, tried to make some changes, and have been grateful for a friend who would speak like that to me. And this was near the end of my time there! For I too am comfortable with leaving things be lest we rock the boat and cause trouble.

How They Found Significance

Any psychologist, including a Christian psychologist, will tell you that we were made to feel significant. Dale Carnegie, author of *How to Win Friends and Influence People*, says the strongest urge in the human race is the desire to feel important. We were made this way. A person who does not find significance will end up with all sorts of problems, including severe emotional problems.

The question is: How do we find significance? The answer is: in God. If we don't find our significance in God, namely in His Son Jesus Christ, we will be pursuing unjust goals—the problem with God's ancient people. "I was enraged by his *sinful greed*," a Hebrew word, as we saw in Chapter 5 that essentially means "unjust goals" (Isa. 57:17). I have done this so many times I blush to think about it.

And that was much of the reason for the Pharisees' problems. Mind you, they did not think there was a problem in the first place. But there were very serious problems indeed and one of them was that they sought to achieve significance in being admired. "They loved to be greeted in the marketplaces and to have men call them 'Rabbi' " (Matt. 23:7). "They loved praise from men more than praise from God" (John 12:43). That was the essence of their comfort zone: being applauded, being complimented, being respected, and being openly referred to. Do this and you had no problem with them. Jesus didn't and had problems with them. These pious men were right in the middle of the conspiracy to have Jesus crucified (John 11:45–51).

Is it not amazing to discover how some people who on the surface seem so godly can become so mean when you cross them? Religious people are the meanest people in the world. Let them remain undisturbed in their comfort zones and they are as sweet as the godfather of the Mafia with his grandchildren. But cross them? Oh dear.

They further sought significance like this: They compared themselves with others—always people they could safely label sinners. That way they always came out on top. So in the aforementioned parable the Pharisee boasted of his good works, then added: "God, I thank you that I am not like other men—robbers, evildoers, adulterers—or even like this tax collector" (Luke 18:11). We can all find someone less righteous to whom we can compare ourselves and therefore come out smelling like a rose. "Comparisons are odious," said Shakespeare, referring to comparisons of one person against another; yet it is perhaps even more odious when we do this to make ourselves look good—"At least I'm not as bad as so-and-so."

The Pharisees even did this when it came to the sainted dead. They piously lamented that the great men of God of the past—prophets, for example—were not appreciated in their own day, some were even persecuted. They would lead the way in extolling the virtues of these great people of yore and proved it by building tombs for them and decorating their graves. Who else was doing this? No one. "No one else cares," said the Pharisees. But we do. We will even have annual conferences and intelligent lectures that show today's generation what really ought to be happening. Moreover, "If we had lived in the days of our forefathers, we would not have taken part with them in shedding the blood of the prophets" (Matt. 23:30). They believed they were not only a cut above today's professing believers, they were better than anyone else in previous generations. In this way they found significance.

They also got their sense of significance in the way they dressed. Said Jesus: "Everything they do is done for men to see: They make their phylacteries wide and the tassels on their garments long" (Matt. 23:5). Dress is very important to a Pharisee; always has been, always will be. They will not be the slightest bit convicted over holding a grudge or speaking evil of fellow believers, but they go to great pains to look good. To look nice, more than nice. So people will say, "I love that suit. I love that dress. I love your hair."

Louise and I will never forget attending the large Baptist convention in Dallas, Texas, in 1985. By then both of us had become very proper and British and were not prepared for the advice a dear friend gave Louise: "Bring at least two sets of clothes for each day. And you might want to bring different colors of nail polish to go with the various outfits. Most of the women take that little bit of extra time to coordinate their colors that way."

My district superintendent in my old denomination was known for his "radical preaching." He preached against women wearing make-up, sleeveless blouses, short hairstyles. In one camp meeting he was one of two preachers; the other was a Scot who deeply impacted me and reportedly came with ten sermons and one suit. They said my old district superintendent came to that camp meeting to preach with ten suits and one sermon. I used to admire him—before he died a few years later living with another man's wife. Jesus called it straining out a gnat and swallowing a camel (Matt. 23:24). Perhaps not your typical Pharisee because I would like to think that most people who have legalistic tendencies are at least moral men and women. But the funny thing is, this particular man is the very one who told my dad I would "eat dust" because I stood with Billy Ball back in 1956.

The Pharisees had a serious problem when it came to money. When Jesus spoke about money (the case can be made He had more to say about this than anything else), the Pharisees became uncomfortable. When He said we cannot serve two masters, either we will hate the one and love the other or be devoted to the one and despise the other because we "cannot serve both God and money." The Pharisees "sneered" at Jesus. And Luke tells us why: They loved money (Luke 16:14). The King James Version translates *philargurus* as "covetous," and virtually the same word is used in 1 Timothy 6:10 when Paul said that the "love of money is the root of all evil." The point is, the Pharisees were motivated by the love of money.

We are talking about the chief enemies of Jesus—who saw right through them—who found their significance in what people said positively about them, by comparing themselves with others and by their very appearance. I wonder how many preachers today need the good suit or clerical garb just to look successful in order to feel important and significant. If I am not careful I will end up a Pharisee in judging them, but I know so many give the impression, even if unintentionally, that their appearance is an essential ingredient to their sense of significance.

Motivation

How do you persuade a Pharisee to give to the poor? The answer is very simple: Hire a couple of trumpeters (a band would be better) and get every one's attention with the music. They announced their giving by the sound of trumpets in the synagogues and on the streets for one reason: "to be honored by men" (Matt. 6:2). And how do you suppose you get a Pharisee to pray? Jesus said, "They love to pray" (Matt. 6:5). If Jesus had said only that they love to pray he would have complimented them. I love to pray. Do you love to pray? Nothing wrong with loving to pray, that's good. But with the Pharisees, "They love to pray standing in the synagogues and on the street corners to be seen by men" (Matt. 6:5). The way you get them to stop praying is to walk away while they are doing it. For there is no motivation left if no one is noticing.

And since we know that Pharisees fasted twice a week, what do you suppose lay behind that worthy practice? They made sure you saw them. First, they looked somber, a practice that may not have been too hard for some Pharisees to carry off. Second, they disfigured their faces—they put on a facial expression that told you they were carrying heavy-duty burdens; this was important stuff, mind you. They didn't even comb their hair when they skipped a meal or two because otherwise you might not notice. Read it all in Matthew 6:1–18.

They were starving for recognition. As long as they got credit for giving, praying or fasting, you could count on them—every time. Take away the credit, the tax exemption, the plaque on the wall, the public knowledge of a generous donation, the thanks before all for doing the flowers in front of the pulpit or for washing up in the church kitchen and there won't be many lining up wanting to help. Pharisees don't particularly enjoy working behind the scenes, driving someone to church when nobody knows about it, visiting the sick without telling it, or giving until their pockets are empty when only God takes notice.

A lady came up to see Louise and me in Fort Lauderdale once to say she had been visiting those who were housebound all week.

"Wonderful," I said. "That's great."

She said she got so much joy in doing this.

"We believe you," we replied.

And then with a straight face she said, "The greatest joy is in not telling it."

The problem with Pharisees is they so often have no objectivity about themselves. This is because their main problem is that they have no sense of sin. None. Sin to them is always in what you do or don't do. Not what you think or feel. It is all outward appearance. They forgot that God looks on the heart (1 Sam. 16:7).

Priorities

The theological assumptions and priorities of Pharisees can be quickly summed up: Their theology was more important than people. They really didn't care about people. It was all theology. Hold to the truth. Contend for the faith. Keep the party line. Above all, remember the Sabbath. Yes. The Sabbath.

> "But my word, dear Pharisee, a blind person was healed."
>
> "Oh yes, but it happened on the Sabbath," comes the terse retort.
>
> "You don't seem to understand, a miracle has taken place. A person who was born blind and has never seen can now see!"
>
> "But *you* don't understand," says the Pharisee with as much warmth as you can find in an igloo. "Truth is at stake here. Something has gone terribly wrong if a person is healed on the Sabbath. Therefore we cannot rejoice when error is clearly being upheld."

Read it for yourself in John 9. Not a single person seemed to be blessed that a blind man could now see. All they could think about was theology. It is almost hilarious that Jesus again and again seemed to wait for the Sabbath before he healed people. Read Matthew 12:2; Mark 2:24; Luke 6:2, 6 and Luke 14:3 for a start. You get the picture that he sees a needy person but says to himself, "It's only two more days until the Sabbath is here and I will wait in order to heal this person then." In other words, Jesus attacked the Pharisees not for their upholding the Law but for putting their traditions and party lines alongside Holy Scripture as if they were of the same authority. There isn't a single word in the Law that says a person should not be made well on the Sabbath.

Not only did they not care about people, they "tie up heavy

loads and put them on men's shoulders, but they themselves are not willing to lift a finger to move them" (Matt. 23:4). They were great at giving orders. They told people what to do. It did not seem to bother them that they could get people around them to do this and yet they themselves did not get their hands dirty. This is why Jesus said, "They do not practice what they preach" (Matt. 23:3).

How They Perpetuated Their Comfort Zone

You may ask, "How could they do this and not feel any conscience about it? How can they sleep at night?" The answer is what I said above: They had no sense of sin. Sin to them is not what you think, it is what you do. This is why Jesus explained the Law as He did: If you hate, you have already committed murder in your heart; if you lusted after a woman (or caused her to lust), you have committed adultery in your heart (Matt. 5:21, 28). But they could not see it that way. This is why they hated all that Jesus preached and did. He did not hold to the party line. They never saw their own sin, ever, as far as we can tell. This is why Jesus said that it was the tax collector, so looked down on by the Pharisee, who was justified before God rather than the Pharisee. "But the tax collector stood at a distance. He would not even look up to heaven, but beat his breast and said, 'God, have mercy on me, a sinner'" (Luke 18:13–14).

They further perpetuated their comfort zones by loopholes they somehow found that set them free from the kind of obedience they were uncomfortable with. The fences that they erected that supposedly protected the Law actually served in some cases to give a way out *not* to obey the Law strictly at all! Jesus nailed them to the wall in this area. The commandment to honor both father and mother was undeniable—this being the fifth commandment. But they had a way of keeping their parents from receiving money that ought to go to them by a rule that enabled them to divert it to the temple or synagogue instead.

> You [Pharisees] say that if a man says to his father or mother, " 'Whatever help you might otherwise have received from me is a gift devoted to God [the money should go to the Lord instead in this case],' he is not to 'honor his father' with it. Thus you nullify the word of God for the sake of your tradition." (Matt. 15:5–6)

When Jesus said that one cannot enter the kingdom of heaven unless one's righteousness actually surpasses that of the Pharisees, nobody could believe their ears. For the ordinary Jew living at the time thought they were so far beneath a Pharisee; the thought of exceeding the righteousness of a Pharisee seemed over the top. But Jesus knew exactly what He was talking about; not only are we justified by faith in Jesus who perfectly fulfilled the Law in our behalf but our very righteousness, when we follow Jesus, far outdistances that of the Pharisee. For the Pharisee never felt any conscience about speaking evil of another, hurting their reputation, holding a grudge, or not forgiving an enemy.

Jesus knew this. He knew that talk about sin in the heart is what they loathed and despised (see Matt. 15:10-20). It is not what *enters* a person's mouth that makes them unclean; it is what *comes out* of it. It is not what enters the stomach and goes out of the body that defiles a person; it is what comes from the heart which makes them unclean. "For out of the heart come evil thoughts, murder, adultery, sexual immorality, theft, false testimony, slander" (Matt. 15:19).

When a man or woman has no sense of inward sin, they predictably have no objectivity about themselves. They are utterly blind to their own minds, their assumptions and motives; they become un-teachable. Jesus called them "blind" (Matt. 23:19). A person of mediocre intelligence with a sense of inward sin by the illumination of the Holy Spirit will have more objectivity about himself or herself, and will certainly be easier to live with, than a highly educated church member who can think only legalistically and see things as black or white. Blindness to our own sin takes away common sense, basic politeness, and care for people's feelings. "But the truth must be defended!" they reply. One thing you can surely say about Pharisees—they aren't very nice!

We are getting closer to the answer to the questions posed above: since Pharisees were vanguards for the Law and were moral and sound on many essential matters, why didn't Jesus congratulate them? Why was He so hard on them? Even if He saw through them, that they were phony in their righteousness, why didn't He leave them alone and attack wicked tax collectors, harlots, and drunkards?

The answer is: They did so much harm. They converted people over to their party line and made that person "twice as much a son of hell as you are" (Matt. 23:15). People like this get more excited over changing a person's theology to suit their own than they do about leading a person to Christ. They will spend more time attacking an enemy who threatens them than going into the world to save the lost. It is like King Saul who was more worried about young David than he was the archenemy of Israel—the Philistines. This is how lopsided people can get and why Jesus knew the Pharisees were dangerous. They did harm to people.

One of the hardest things Jesus said to them was this: "You shut the kingdom of heaven in men's faces. You yourselves do not enter, nor will you let those enter who are trying to" (Matt.

23:13–14). This is basically what happened to that couple I referred to earlier who sailed all the way from India to England in 1904 to see the Welsh Revival but returned to India without going to Wales, because of their friends' bias against it. I have seen this happen too often. I have watched innocent people forfeit blessing that would have been theirs because a "mature" Christian put them off from pursuing God.

John warned, "Watch out that you do not lose what you have worked for, but that you may be rewarded fully" (2 John 8). This verse is to be applied to one who has made great spiritual progress in their faith—and is well on their way to receiving a reward—but who is still vulnerable to older and "wiser" people who might actually do them harm. Sadly, there are Pharisees around who spend more time lecturing to zealous new Christians and trying to change their theological views than being concerned about the world going to hell. People like this are not soul winners; they invariably fish in the Christian pond to change one's doctrinal point of view.

The hardest era Louise and I ever endured at Westminster Chapel was when we observed younger Christians being told by certain older members not to come to the Chapel because the minister (me) wasn't a true man of God. This occurred after I brought Arthur Blessitt to preach at the chapel. Visitors would come to hear me preach but would be approached by some of our older members who would say, "There's trouble here; this is not the church for you," so many of these people wouldn't come back.

We knew one man who was converted literally in and from the gutter and was delivered from drunkenness and poverty who eventually fell to this kind of opposition to my ministry. We knew him well and used to talk a lot. His face was aglow with his new faith. He loved me—I could feel it. I would never have dreamed of this possibility in a thousand years, but because I did not "dot the i's or cross the t's" as some legalistic people required of me, this man was warned against me and actually turned away. He began going to another church. That part was okay by me, though I was of course disappointed. But he didn't stay long in his new church, although I never found out why. He needed new friends there, for one thing. I only know that the last I heard he ended up back in the world and in the gutter, and died in that state. I would justly call people Pharisees who oppose what they do not like in a church because it does not fall within their cherished tradition. These will "not let those enter who are trying to."

Therefore if you ask, "why would Jesus not appreciate the Pharisees but single them out as enemies when they would seem to be on the right side of the issue?," the answer again is that they did so much harm. Then and now. Jesus knew they needed to be warned against. On one occasion He paired them with Herod. " 'Be careful,' Jesus warned them. 'Watch out for the yeast of the Pharisees and that of Herod' " (Mark 8:15). The disciples didn't understand at first but it eventually sunk in—"he was not telling them to guard against the yeast used in bread, but against the teaching of the Pharisees" (Matt. 16:12). It therefore wasn't personal; they were to guard against the teaching of these people. People are people. But if they imbibe unhealthy teaching they turn into monsters.

But Jesus also knew that Pharisees would be the ones who would lead the way to His own death. There was never a thought that such a conspiracy would be instigated by the notorious sinners of the day, those who were drunkards, whoremongers, adulterers, or even murderers. Not that they were incapable of such a crime, but, generally speaking, people like that don't tend to send an innocent man to the cross. Religious people do. Jesus therefore had their number and declared war on them from almost the first time he opened His mouth. "Do not think that I have come to abolish the Law," He said early on in the Sermon on the Mount (Matt. 5:17). Why say that? Why bring that subject up? It was because Jesus wanted to get to the heart of the matter as soon as possible. When He began to attack their interpretations of the Law He knew He would be in a constant battle with them from then on. It worked. They led the way in getting Him crucified. But that is what He came to do! He came to die on the cross for our sins and, in the meantime, establish the kind of people who would be saved. "I have not come to call the righteous [by which he meant those who purport to be righteous], but sinners to repentance" (Luke 5:32).

Outside Their Comfort Zone

What Threatened Them

The main thing that threatened Pharisees was any success enjoyed by those who did not uphold their party line. Keep in mind that the Pharisees were a party within Judaism. They wanted prestige and glory for their own party and party line. They feared being outnumbered and were therefore threatened by the common people taking so fondly to Jesus. Some thought that Jesus really was the promised Messiah. This really upset Pharisees. Therefore, if Jesus enjoyed any measure of undoubted success (though Jesus was not trying to be "successful" as such)—whether by growing crowds or performing a miracle—the Pharisees were then thrust right out of their comfort zones.

It was basically a matter of jealousy, of course. Jealousy—the sin we never see in ourselves but readily seen when others have it—always intensifies when someone is pushed suddenly and without warning outside their comfort zone. When someone chooses to go outside their comfort zone because of obedience to the Lord, it is a different matter; jealousy has greater difficulty growing. But when we are threatened by another's anointing, as Saul was threatened by David (1 Sam. 18:12), our insecurity grows. Fear spreads from the crown of our heads to the soles of our feet. This is what was happening to Pharisees every time Jesus opened His mouth or performed another miracle.

Even Pontius Pilate knew that "it was out of envy that the chief priests had handed Jesus over to him" (Mark 15:10). They were threatened by the miracles. They were threatened by Jesus' treatment of the Law and his doctrine of sin, and were of course threatened by not achieving significance from the applause of people. But what really got their goat was having to watch someone outside their own party winning the hearts of the people.

"The common people heard him gladly" (Mark 12:37 KJV). On one occasion (see John 7:45–49), they sent a temple guard to bring Jesus in so they could arrest him. But these guards came back shortly, but without Jesus. "Why didn't you bring him in?" they were asked.

The guards replied, "No one ever spoke the way this man does."

"You mean he has deceived you also?" the Pharisees retorted.

This sort of thing thrust Pharisees right out of their comfort zone. They resorted to their theology: "this mob [the people following Jesus] . . . knows nothing of the law." Their ultimate weapon against common Jews was the threat of putting out of the synagogue anyone who confessed faith in Jesus (John 12:42). The typical ploy of a Pharisee is to motivate by fear.

Their attack lay in the idea of "guilt by association." This tactic was used by Pharisees then and continues to be used today. If people who are attracted to you—or people you spend time with—are unworthy, theologically inarticulate, not of good stock or of respectable credentials, all of you are in the same boat together and should be regarded as being cut out of the same cloth. You are all equally guilty. You prove your guilt by those with whom you are friendly.

The Pharisees' trump card therefore: The kind of people that Jesus allowed to be around Him, the quality of people affirming Him and the backgrounds of those who were brought closest to Him. "This man welcomes sinners and eats with them" (Luke 15:2). This, to the Pharisees, should be enough to indict Jesus as one to be shunned; surely this would cause everybody to turn against Jesus. But it didn't work. Jesus even pleaded guilty to the charge and told several more parables (Luke 15 and 16) to show that the Father loves and welcomes sinners into His family.

Pharisees yesterday and today love to repudiate a person by the quality of the people they seek to reach or those who admire them. Jesus surprised everybody by choosing a tax collector to be one of the twelve disciples. That was just not right! The Pharisees, on the other hand, quickly wrote off those who mixed with non-adherents to their party line.

I received a letter from a man who ended it with, "May God have mercy on your soul," which I doubt he really wanted for me, because I spent time with Yasser Arafat and tried to lead this leader to Christ. I was charged with guilt by association, but I knew Jesus would go into Ramallah. One of the closest friends I ever had broke with me because I accepted a preaching invitation of which he did not approve. His reason was that it did not make him look good. Since I was known to be close to him, it did not suit him for me to be seen preaching to that particular group of Christians. Again, it was guilt by association.

I had a close ministerial friend who refused to go into a bar to witness for Jesus. "Why?" I asked.

"Because someone might see me go in and think I was there to have a drink," he said.

I said to him, "Surely your life is such that people would never question why you would be there. Jesus would not care what people thought but would be right in the middle of that bar talking to sinners."

He eventually took my advice and has since thanked me. He began to see God work in his ministry when he did not worry about his reputation. Reputation means everything to a Pharisee who is looking over his shoulder all the time to see who is watching. The Pharisees wanted to preserve the Law, their fence around the Law, and the reputation of their forefathers who they thought were the last to see God work powerfully in Israel.

The Pharisees were at home when praising the great men of God of the past but threatened by the thought that God was doing something now. That God would be at work today and putting them right outside their comfort zones. For all of us today it is great indeed to hear of wonderful revivals of the past, of men of God who did marvelous and courageous things two hundred years ago, or perhaps only fifty years ago. But not today. We are in our comfort zones talking about what God did yesterday. But talk of God doing something today, unless it is on some remote island in the Third World, is too threatening a topic. Anyone who says that what is happening now is of God will be treated with disbelief.

This was part of the offense when Jesus, stood and read from Isaiah 61:1–2, then sat down and declared, "*Today* this scripture is fulfilled in your hearing" (Luke 4:18–21). It was of great offense when Peter, speaking on the day of Pentecost, said that what was going on before their very eyes was the fulfillment of the prophet Joel's words (Acts 2:16ff.). Any reckoning that God is at work *now* makes us all uneasy; the Pharisaism that lies beneath the surface breaks out in fear and suspicion.

Pharisees are even threatened by those who actually do not pose a real threat to them at all. For example, children. The ire of self-righteousness will rise in the Pharisee when children lose their heads and get involved in worshipping Jesus. This happened on Palm Sunday. "But when the chief priests and teachers of the law saw the wonderful things he did and the children shouting in the temple area, 'Hosanna to the Son of David,' they were indignant" (Matt. 21:15). What do children know? How much theological training could they have received? What's more, these children were shouting! That sort of thing always makes religious people uneasy. When we see kids—or any young person—getting carried away under the inspiration of worship and praise, we get very uncomfortable. We are afraid things will get out of hand. I have watched God move powerfully over the years when the children get involved. I have often thought that the next move of God on earth will witness children and young people doing mighty things for the Lord—possibly even leading the way.

How They Reacted

When a Pharisee is outside his comfort zone he has to do something. One of the main things: He accuses and says, "This is not of God." Sometimes he crosses over a line and says, "This is of the devil." This is a dangerous thing to do. When this was done in presence of Jesus and the very miraculous, He introduced a very scary teaching—the sin for which there is no forgiveness. He called it blasphemy against the Holy Spirit which makes a person guilty of an "eternal sin"—all because they were saying of Jesus, "He has an evil spirit" (Mark 3:28–30).

Why is it that some of us are more willing to accept that it is the devil at work than we are that something or someone is actually of God? If we have a party line that says, "God doesn't do the miraculous nowadays—that ended after the closing of the canon of Scripture," we are forced to explain what is happening. To be on the safe side we may say a miracle takes place by a psychological reaction (this is what some said when Louise in her weakest and darkest hour was prayed for by Rodney Howard-Browne—and was instantaneously healed). But I know of some who accused Rodney of preaching in a tongue that was demonic and out of the dark regions of Africa. Whoever said it first, I don't know; I only know I would not want to be in their shoes. It is one thing to be outside your comfort zone because of reports of the miraculous which you don't understand; it is crossing well over the line to say it is of Satan. Whatever you say, don't say that.

It is sad but sobering to realize how far we will go to defend our party line. We get defensive. Say crazy things. Get very suspicious. Send out spies, like those Jews who were sent from Jerusalem to investigate John the Baptist (John 1:19). Anyone who puts us outside our comfort zone—such as a man whose clothes were made of camel's hair with a leather belt around his waist, and calling for repentance—becomes our next target. Before it is all over we even turn on the man who was actually healed. That's what happened to the lad who was healed of blindness. Though he ought to have had a chance to enjoy his sight for a while, he was instead having to explain himself and was eventually persecuted—just because he was the one healed (John 9:26–34).

Those Pharisees who are thrust outside their comfort zones seem to live for the moment when they can trap the one who threatens them, catch them in an unguarded comment or find something that enables them to say "Gotcha!" What a way to live: using your time and energy to hope someone will make a comment by which they can be labeled heretic or, at least, be embarrassed. Pharisees yesterday and today live for this. "Then the Pharisees went out and laid plans to trap him in his words" (Matt. 22:15). When they found the woman in the act of adultery they used their questions about her "as a trap, in order to have a basis for accusing him" (John 8:3–6). The moment they hope for: When they can make another lose face and be caught. People like this are not happy with themselves but will continue on unless God mercifully reaches down and touches their hearts—as in the case of Nicodemus or Saul of Tarsus. That means there is the hope for all of us who are plagued by a pharisaical weakness.

The worst thing of all, however, was this. The Pharisees' search for significance outside God and from the praise of people lay at the bottom of their inability to recognize God's Messiah when He stood before their very eyes. Have you wondered why ancient Israel missed out when the Messiah came? Have you wondered why they still reject Him? I can tell you. It is because they chose the immediate gratification of receiving praise from people rather than to seek honor that comes only from God. Seeking the honor, praise, and glory that comes from God alone means letting go of the applause of men and women. It also means a lot of patience, because you don't feel anything the first day when you make this a lifelong pursuit. So it isn't easy. The Pharisees simply weren't going to go that route; it was too hard. Surely their reverence for the Law was good enough. The Law is God's product; the Law isn't God himself. And those who give priority to the Law inevitably end up as Pharisees and miss out on God's next move, just as the Jews missed out on their own Messiah.

Therefore Jesus was not surprised at their refusal to believe in Him. He gave the explanation Himself and summed up their unbelief in a simple question He asked: "How can you believe if you accept praise from one another, yet make no effort to obtain the praise that comes from the only God?" (John 5:44). They made a choice: They preferred compliments, adoration, admiration, and glory from people. Jesus said they "made no effort" to see what it would have been like had they sought their significance in the sheer glory of God. But they opted for the glory of man. This felt better. Possibly, for a while. But at the end of the day one who makes this choice will pay for it dearly and suffer for it bitterly—forever—unless God mercifully steps down as He did in the cases of Nicodemus and Saul of Tarsus. And me. And I hope you.

What breaks your heart is that the Pharisees were the ones who led to Jesus' weeping over the city of Jerusalem, in a lengthy denunciation of the Pharisees in Matthew 23. It culminated in Jesus crying out,

> O Jerusalem, Jerusalem, you who kill the prophets and stone those sent to you, how often I have longed to gather your children together, as a hen gathers her chicks under her wings, but you were not willing. Look, your house is left to you desolate. (Matt. 23:37–38)

·6·

Twenty-Five Reasons You May Be a Pharisee

> It is a test of a good religion whether you can joke about it.
>
> G. K. CHESTERTON

A few years ago someone sent me a humorous booklet of cartoons entitled *You Might Be a Redneck If* by Jeff Foxworthy. A redneck is someone who never lies in the sun to get a tan but is always fiery red on the back of his neck because he wears a tee shirt and works in the sun. He is associated with ignorance and virtually no culture. The booklet is written to get people to see that they might just be a redneck if certain things apply to them, such as: You take a load to the garbage dump and bring back more than you took; you had to remove your toothpick for your wedding pictures; your dad walks you to school because you're both in the same grade; you think Sherlock Holmes is a housing project in Mississippi.

My colleague Jack Taylor used a phrase in a sermon, "Chances are you are a Pharisee if" and I have been intrigued by the idea ever since. We all need to learn to laugh at ourselves and not be defensive when our weakness is touched on. Meekness, a great virtue, could be defined as the ability to accept a hard criticism without being the slightest bit defensive. A certain measure of meekness is required to work through this chapter because I think it hits all of us. I lead the way, I assure you, in being an expert in Pharisaism because too much that follows continues to hit me between the eyes. I am not proud of this. But I want you to know I do not see myself as being fully emancipated from this bondage. And yet we are going to look further at the very sins that angered our Lord Jesus most.

Sometimes we get angry at church, even in a prayer meeting. Prayer meetings are the backbone of a good church but can also be the most painfully boring times of the week. This is because there are those who love to hear themselves pray—and drive others mad. My friend Harry Kilbride, who lives not far from us in Florida, told me of two incidents in one of his former churches in which people had to be lovingly rebuked for their long prayers. In one case, a man would pray the same prayer week after week, and it went on and on before getting to the petitions: "We praise thee, O God, for thy love, thy sovereignty, thy omnipotence, this wonderful salvation you have given in sending thy Son . . ." On and on the man would go.

Harry knew this man kept others from praying and also was in danger of making people run away, especially young people whom he wanted to encourage to come. So he made a public appeal to those who came that perhaps not everybody should pray every single week. The man never came back to the prayer meeting again. It seems he did not care to be truly involved in prayer unless he could pray his long prayers.

The second incident had to do with a lady who prayed much the same way. In this case Dr. Kilbride asked her to see him in the vestry. He asked if she enjoyed the prayer meetings and how she thought they were going. "Oh wonderful, pastor," she said. He then, as gently as he could—sugar-coating the medicine—asked her if perhaps she might pray not every single week but perhaps once every three weeks, in order to encourage others, especially young people, to pray also. The woman agreed. The problem was, after that, she only came once every three weeks—and she would then pray! She too was not interested in coming unless she prayed.

These are examples of how Pharisees, though good people in so many ways, are alive and well in the Church today. In Westminster Chapel we had a sweet old lady (now in heaven) who prayed aloud every time there was a prayer meeting and would not finish a prayer without condemning those who weren't present. "Lord, you know there are so few of us here. So many don't care to come to a prayer meeting. So many don't love you. They don't want to carry the load. They don't want to intercede . . ." On and on she would go. It had the effect of making all present sigh the moment she began, and we wished she could somehow manage to pray without pointing the finger. It is a subtle form of Pharisaism. It is a religious spirit, one of the hardest nuts to crack in the Church today. It is the enemy of what God wants to do in the here and now.

If, however, Pharisaism makes us angry when we see it in others, we need to see it in ourselves and how it must equally grieve the Holy Spirit. Jesus' words perfectly mirrored what the Father wanted said (John 5:19), and we can be equally sure that the Holy Spirit, who is the Spirit of Christ, feels the same things Jesus felt. And yet it is easy to see it in others; can we see this in ourselves?

This is why this chapter is important. If certain aspects of the Pharisees raised the holy ire of the Son of God, who was devoid of self-righteousness, I want to be sure I am convicted of pharisaism in my own heart and life and am doing everything I possibly can to not be like the ancient Pharisees of Jesus' day.

What is the possibility that you and I could be a Pharisee? What are the signs—or warning signals? Chances are you and I are Pharisees if:

1. *We love to point the finger.* It comes easily. And the devil does it best. He is called "the accuser" (Rev. 12:10). You must choose whether you want to play the devil and point the finger or be Jesus who lets us save face. Jesus actually gave us a selfish motivation for not pointing the finger. "Do not judge, and you will not be judged" (Luke 6:37). I will forfeit the benefit of this promise if I play the role of accuser. On the other hand, if I choose the pointing of the finger rather than let God sort out the person I want to condemn, I too "will be judged" (Matt. 7:1). Believe me, I know this to be true by experience! It is safe and far better to cease pointing the finger—ever again. You will never be sorry.

2. *We love to say "Gotcha."* We love to catch the person in the act whereby they cannot deny they got caught. Or to get to see them squirm when they are found out. It is said that a journalist's dream is to write an article or book in order to say "Gotcha"—like finding someone highly respected, such as Billy Graham or Mother Theresa, and exposing their imperfections. God knows we all have skeletons in the cupboard and if He decided to tell the world what He knows about us we would die on the spot. But there is a better way to live. Joseph fantasized that he would see the dream fulfilled of his brothers bowing down to him, after the wicked thing they did to him, and say "Gotcha" to them. But when the dream was actually fulfilled he was a changed man and, instead of looking at them with glee in their helpless state, he wept over them and totally forgave them (Gen. 45:1–11). That was the secret of his greatness and the reason God trusted him with such a lofty status.

3. *We are good at sending people on a guilt trip.* The Law invariably finds people guilty. When you have interpretations of the Law that exceed the Law—or rules of your own you think are valid—it only widens the scope for the possibility of guilt. And when we superimpose our rules and wishes on friends or enemies in order to require that they come up to our standard we become Pharisees. They loved to make people feel guilty. God is not that way. Believe it or not, once we are justified by faith in Christ alone and walking by faith, God does not want any of us to feel guilty. On the contrary, He gives us the Holy Spirit whereby we say to him, "*Abba*, Father" (Rom. 8:15). When the guilt is gone and we have fellowship with the Father, the joy is greater than any this world can offer. Total forgiveness means we do not send another person on a guilt trip; we are aware of what we have been forgiven and we treat others as God has treated us.

4. *We require standards of people not written in Scripture.* I grew up in a church in which they often spoke of standards. Godly standards. I could not go to the movies as a child. My mother did not wear lipstick. My father would not read a Sunday newspaper. I could not play ball on Sunday. Some preachers in my old denomination seemed to try to outdo each other on how strict you could be. I always felt sorry for the teenage girls in my church because they were the only ones in their school who could not wear makeup. When we impose rules on people—even though we might justify them for some reason or another—that are not solidly written in the Word of God, we risk being the Pharisees of our day. It only adds to people's bondage. I urged members of Westminster Chapel to pray thirty minutes a day but it was never a requirement. It was not a rule, only a suggestion. But standards are rules that people must live by—or be "out" rather than "in." God does not like this. Pharisees do.

5. *We practice guilt by association.* We accuse people of being unclean, unrighteous, or out of order when they mix with people of other faiths, varying views, or questionable lifestyles. If I accept an invitation to preach to a group with whom I do not agree theologically, does it make me guilty of condoning what they believe? No. But some would accuse me. Pharisees would. Not Jesus. If I invite a person to preach for me but who happens to hold to views I am uncomfortable with, does this make me guilty by having this person in my pulpit? No. If I pray with a fellow Christian who is not totally at one with me doctrinally does that make me guilty by associating with them in this way? No. But if I accuse you of being a sinner because you are having a meal with a sinner, then I am a Pharisee. If I try to make you feel shameful because of who you choose to spend time with, I am a Pharisee.

6. *We assume something or someone is of the devil when their ministry makes us uncomfortable.* The Pharisees could not deny that Jesus performed miracles. If they said that these miracles were done by God it would have condoned Jesus' behavior and put them to shame. So they resorted to a trick that has been repeated many times since: They attributed what was done to the devil. In this even Martin Luther became a Pharisee. He actually once said of his rival, Ulrich Zwingli (1484–1531), "Zwingli's God is my devil" because of differing views regarding the Lord's Supper. If you and I are threatened by someone's success and notice how popular they are but have no answer but to say, "They are of the devil," we are Pharisees. It is fair to say they are misguided or in theological error. But to claim they are of the devil is dangerous stuff. If you or I ever say this we had better be right. The Pharisees had no hesitation and neither do modern Pharisees who resort to the ultimate put-down in order to make their opponents look bad. Jesus would not do that.

7. *We say a person is not a Christian if they disagree with us.* That is judging just like the Pharisees did. It is a quick cop-out, it is our way of punishing the person with whom we disagree. Instead of saying politely that they for some reason disagree with us we glibly say, "These people aren't even saved." There is always the possibility in some cases of course that those who attack us are not truly converted. But why say that? Why not give them the benefit of the doubt? Why resort to the ultimate insult just because they don't agree with us? It is almost childish to label a person an unbeliever just because we don't agree. Even if they are unsaved, if we treat them with love and dignity, they may be converted one day and will love and respect us for the way we treated them in the meantime. A good rule of thumb: When you fall out with a person, treat them with such dignity that they will respect you when you make up. Pharisees don't want to make up with people.

8. *We esteem "the way we've always done it" above change, even when the latter is not heretical.* Remember that the Pharisees made the Word of God of no effect by their traditions (Matt. 15:6). Their own traditions were based not on Scripture but their peculiar rules. When new ways emerge but which are not contrary to Scripture, beware of falling into the trap of always wanting the old wine. Those who say, "The old is better" (Luke 5:39) want to stay in their comfort zones—to keep the taste they are used to. All new movements God raises up require change. Every person described in Hebrews 11 had to move out of their comfort zones. They broke with tradition. At Westminster Chapel I had a fight on my hands because I wanted the organist to play "Turn Your Eyes upon Jesus" as a prelude rather than Mozart. The latter, I was told—and not by the organist—made our Willis pipe organ sound better. My old friend and assistant Jon Bush used to say

that the last seven words of a dying church were: "We never did it that way before."

9. *We do not practice what we preach.* Jesus plainly said of Pharisees that they "do not practice what they preach" (Matt. 23:3). I cannot think of a greater hypocrisy on the planet than demanding of another person what I would not do myself. What turned Gandhi against Christianity was Christians. The greatest testimony we could give to the world is not our articulate theology or eloquent way of presenting it but their discovery that we are real—that we really do practice what we preach. This does not mean we are perfect or never sin. "If we claim to be without sin, we deceive ourselves and the truth is not in us" (1 John 1:8). But if our faces, hearts, and lives reflect the love of Jesus, people are going to want what we've got. As a Muslim businessman said to Arthur Blessitt in a bar in Jordan, "I want what you've got"—referring to Arthur's countenance.

'Twas not the truth you taught, to you so clear,
to me so dim;
But when you came to me you brought a sense of
Him.
Yes from your eyes He beckoned me, and from
your heart His love was shed,
And I lost sight of you and saw the Christ instead.

ANONYMOUS

10. *We are more comfortable talking about the mighty movements of God yesterday than today.* It will be recalled that the Pharisees thought themselves pious and faithful because they decorated the tombs of the prophets. The Pharisees even fancied that they would have recognized God at work and would not have been

critical of what God was doing had they been around in previous generations. It is like saying we would not have crucified Jesus had we been around at that time. This is sheer self-righteousness. We all crucified Jesus. We all are critical of what God is up to in the here and now—it always means going outside our comfort zone—unless He opens our eyes. It is also wrong to dismiss what is happening today because it does not repeat exactly what was happening before. There was no clear precedent that I know of for what characterized the Welsh Revival. In any case, God does not always do the same thing twice. We must be willing to lose face for God's glory and recognize that God may be working right before our eyes. The offense is to say this is God at work now.

11. *We take ourselves too seriously.* The Pharisees thought they were God's remnant and it was up to them to preserve the Law by their traditions. They took themselves very seriously by the attention they demanded, the way they dressed, the way they tried to trap Jesus, demanding to be called "Rabbi," and insisting on seats of honor. This is the lifestyle of a Pharisee and it is not a good sign at all when we take ourselves very seriously. This means we can't laugh at ourselves—certainly we can't cope with being laughed at, listen to criticism without being defensive, or be passed by without sulking when we thought we should be invited. The most secure people are those who can laugh at themselves, accept criticism without being defensive, and be passed over when they think they should have been consulted or invited. The main psychological problem of the Pharisees was that they were insecure.

12. *We judge by outward appearance.* This borders on guilt by association but is slightly different. I refer to when we don't like the way a person dresses—too fashionable, too expensive or too

casual; we don't like their accent—too posh or too working-class; we don't approve of their education or lack of it—or where they received it; we don't approve of their theological or church background; we judge them by their neighborhood; we don't approve of their employment; we don't like their friends. Pharisees are masters at this. People criticized Arthur Blessitt because he wore jeans in our pulpit. I was criticized when I stopped wearing a Geneva gown. These are things that should not come into our minds. Unless we want to be the Pharisees of our day.

It will be recalled that Pharisees strutted around in their garb because "Everything they do is done for men to see," said Jesus (Matt. 23:5). This does not mean we are oblivious to the way we are seen in public. Of course not. I want to look nice. I make sure my hair is combed and that I have had a clean shave. But if I seek significance by my appearance or my clothes or whether or not I wear a suit or tie, I have lapsed into a pharisaical mode that is certainly not good.

13. *We care more about people's opinions than God's.* Jesus said the Jews could not believe in his Messiahship because they preferred the praise of one another rather than making an effort to receive God's praise; the Greek word in John 5:44 is *doxa* which means glory, honor, or praise. It comes from a root word that means "opinion." This means that God has an opinion. We must make a choice: whose opinion matters? If we care more about what people think, we are Pharisees. What is gravely serious about this is the very point I have made: By making no effort to obtain God's praise, or opinion, they set themselves up for unbelief. Thus when the very Messiah they claimed they longed for came and was right under their noses, they did not recognize Him. All because they developed a habit of wanting the praise of people rather than of God. This may seem a fairly innocuous

tendency—since it is surely human to want people to compliment us—but making no effort to obtain His compliment of them ended up cutting off their hope of seeing and enjoying God work in their own day. Speaking personally, of all the points I am listing in this part of the book, this one is the premise I value most of all. I fear more than anything else in the world that I should want your approval of me more than God's.

14. *We need to be sure people know about it if we give, pray, or fast.* You will recall that Jesus told us not to be like those who only gave, prayed, or fasted when it would be seen by other people. Why was this so important? It is important because the principle just looked at above—that of John 5:44—is at stake. Jesus made it clear: If we do what we do to be seen of men we get our reward; yes, but it is only in the here and now—the feeling that builds up our egos: the praise of people, not of God. The irony is, we develop the healthiest egos, significance, and sense of self-esteem when we cultivate a habit of seeking only the praise of God. God has a way of doubling our sense of significance and self-esteem. He will not let us down. But when we choose to give, pray or fast only when people are likely to find out, we risk repeating the fatal sin of the ancient Jews who utterly missed out on what God wanted them to receive. The same missing out can happen today as well.

15. *We are motivated by money.* You will recall that the Pharisees loved money and were motivated by the love of money. It was an important insight by Luke (Luke 16:14). It should not be surprising. For when all else is said about Pharisees it follows that a love of money would be very close by. What will make it easy for us to turn loose our money is the promise of people finding out that we gave! This shows that pride runs almost parallel with

our love of money. In other words, we hang on to our cash and assets, but if someone dangles a promise that our giving, whether to a church or charity, will be known by our getting special recognition and credit, the motivation to give is increased adequately to make us give. God gets no glory in this case, neither do we receive a reward from Him; only the reward that people say, "How good of you to do that." What is more telling, however, is that we spend lavishly on ourselves and feel totally at ease. What we buy adds to our prestige and causes others to feel envious—which we love to think is happening with them.

16. *We feel righteous by comparing ourselves to others.* Rather than measuring ourselves by the Word of God we measure others. Instead of discovering the sinfulness of our own hearts, which is so painful, we immediately find someone nearby who we judge to be in bad shape and assume, by contrast, we are okay. But that is by comparison. Besides, we don't know what is in another's heart. Therefore when we get a righteous feeling by selecting somebody we assume to be more wicked than ourselves, we totally avoid the very things Jesus wants us to do; namely, to see what we are like before God and not in the eyes of people. The tax collector was justified because he felt so unworthy before God (Luke 18:13–14); the Pharisee was not justified because the only way he could feel good was to compare himself to the sinful tax collector. He felt better about himself but had no idea how he appeared before God. This is the very reason a Pharisee lacks objectivity about himself and is so superficial: he gets his smug feeling by finding someone he can look down on—and never gives the matter another thought.

17. *We have no sense of sin by our thoughts, only our deeds.* The Pharisees were offended by the teaching that what makes a per-

son unclean is "what come out of his mouth" rather than what goes in (Matt. 15:11–12). A good rule of thumb in assessing whether we are Pharisees is how we get a sense of sin. If it is only in what we do then we can get off the hook quite a bit. The Pharisees could only conceive of sin in terms of outward acts—as in most of the Ten Commandments. They never dwell on the Tenth Commandment, which has to do with the heart; namely coveting, which is what convinced the righteous Saul of Tarsus that he really was a sinner after all (Rom. 7:7–9).

My own theological background did not prepare me for this most powerful and essential insight—that sin is in our thoughts as well as our deeds. What ultimately convinced me, apart from the conviction through the immediate and direct witness of the Spirit, was John's words, "If we claim to be without sin, we deceive ourselves and the truth is not in us" (1 John 1:8). Therefore if we claim to be without sin, merely because we haven't done anything such as being sexual immoral, we are first self-deceived and second devoid of the truth.

18. *We major on minors.* We do this in a thousand ways of course, but the example Jesus gave when He said that Pharisees "strain out a gnat but swallow a camel" had to do with tithing (Matt. 23:23–24). A Pharisee is one who avoids personal obligation to the whole Law by keeping some of it; namely, rules which give them a good feeling that they are okay. Tithing does this nicely. If someone tithes, they tell themselves they are okay because "Most people don't." Moreover, they make sure they tithe by doing it across the board—tithing spices such as mint, dill, and cumin. Nothing is left out. Never mind that there are weightier matters of the Law—like justice (caring for the poor), mercy (showing kindness to strangers), and faithfulness twenty-four hours a day to the entire world. If we prove that we

tithe, this counts for righteousness somehow (we tell ourselves). I found it was sometimes easier to get Christians to tithe at Westminster Chapel than it was to get them out on the streets witnessing on a Saturday morning—or to totally forgive their enemies. It is like the rules in Jerusalem today. There are those who excuse all manner of sins, but they make sure they uphold dietary laws, such as "Do not cook a young goat in its mother's milk" (Exod. 23:19). When brought forward to today, this means do not put mayonnaise on a beef sandwich.

19. *We are experts in finding loopholes in the Law to excuse certain areas of disobedience.* One of the rules of the ancient Pharisees which was not part of the Law but part of their fence around the Law was a way of avoiding responsibility to parents. Whereas the Law states, "Honor your father and mother," the Pharisees said, "'Whatever help you [the parents] might otherwise have received from me [your son] is a gift devoted to God,' that he is not to 'honor his father' with it" (Matt. 15:5–6). Money that should have been given to parents was diverted to the synagogue or temple. This way the Pharisee could divert money that was to be earmarked for his parents to the synagogue. Thus Jesus said, "You break the command of God for the sake of your tradition" (Matt. 15:3–6). The Pharisee reasoned, "My parents don't need the money but the synagogue does." We can do that today in many ways. For example, my church (the storehouse) doesn't need the money; I need to pay my bills, which God would want me to do. We create our own loopholes. For example, we excuse ourselves from forgiving another because they are not sorry, or they have not apologized, or they need to repent first. Our model is to be Jesus, not the Pharisees. Nobody repented at the sight of the crucifixion, and yet He said, "Father, forgive them, for they do not know what they are doing" (Luke 23:34).

20. *We are more concerned to uphold our theology than to help people.* We saw how the Pharisees could not bring themselves to rejoice that a blind man was healed because the healing took place on the Sabbath. It is good when we hold sound theology high in our priorities. I am a theologian and I love theology. But there comes a time that I must accept that God will use a person who is not in agreement with my thinking. When God uses a person whose theology I could pick to pieces, which is more important—to scold him for his error or rejoice that God uses such a person to see people blessed, healed, and delivered? Not to rejoice in someone being blessed, no matter the instrument God chooses, merely because I don't agree with the person, makes me a Pharisee. God may use one whose theology is different, whose church is different and whose culture is different. I should affirm what God does through a person I may not particularly like.

21. *We love to score theological points with our enemies.* Two of the ancient parties in Judaism were the Pharisees (in some ways the fundamentalists of their day) and the Sadducees (in some ways the liberals of their day). They had in common a hatred for Jesus but each still got their thrills from making their rivals look bad. When the Pharisees noted gleefully that Jesus had silenced the Sadducees with his argument against them regarding resurrection (Matt. 22:34), they immediately wanted to have their turn at challenging Jesus. In other words, while opposing Jesus both Pharisees and Sadducees took shots at each other; this sort of thing got them worked up and excited.

The apostle Paul knew this and played into the rivalry brilliantly when he was being tried. He said before the Sanhedrin that he was on trial because of his hope in the resurrection of the dead. "When he said this, a dispute broke out between the Pharisees and the Sadducees, and the assembly was divided."

The episode got Paul out of a difficult situation and bought him more time (Acts 23:6–10). I am reminded of two churches in Alabama, one Methodist (which believed you could lose your salvation if you sinned), the other Baptist (who believed once saved, always saved). The two churches ran missions concurrently but the Baptists were heard to say later, "Well, we didn't have much of a revival, but thank God the Methodists didn't either." Vintage Pharisaism.

22. *We claim God's approval of us rather than our rivals because we know our theology, not theirs, is sound.* The party spirit that emerged from the rivalry between Sadducees and Pharisees kept them apart and fueled their motivation to score points. But at bottom the Pharisees knew that God must be with them rather than their opponents because of such teachings as the resurrected life beyond the grave and belief in angels. The Sadducees did not believe in these and the Pharisees knew these truths were solidly based in their Law and traditions; therefore God would decidedly be on their side. This gave them a superior feeling. They did not merely think—they knew they were on the side of the angels. It did not seem to bother them at all that right before their eyes was God's very Son who they did not recognize. It is so easy for us to take ourselves so seriously because we know God would be on the side of the party who is sounder. Really? He may well feel toward us as Jesus did the Pharisees.

23. *We easily dismiss a person we don't want to like because we are able to find something truly wrong with them.* This is an old Pharisaical tactic—find something you know is really wrong; therefore you are at utter peace in rejecting that person entirely. The Pharisees found what they were looking for: Jesus

claimed to be able to forgive sins. What? Forgive sins? Blasphemy! Who can forgive sins but God alone? Jesus calmly asked, "Which is easier: to say, 'Your sins are forgiven,' or to say, 'Get up and walk'?" (Luke 5:21–23). We do this too. When we hope we don't have to accept someone we look for something we know is absolutely wrong in them; therefore we have the excuse we need not to affirm them. "He doesn't believe in the Rapture." "This man doesn't believe in the millennium." "This person speaks in tongues." "This person has not been baptized in the Holy Spirit." When we find what we are looking for we tell ourselves, "Don't worry about affirming this person—you know what is seriously wrong in them." I knew of one preacher who rejected Dr. James Kennedy's method of winning souls called Evangelism Explosion because Dr. Kennedy does not believe in a literal one-thousand-year reign of Jesus on the earth after the Second Coming.

24. *We say, "We are more in tune with God than you are."* This works several ways, but let me mention two of them. First, take people known as being charismatic. So many of them, I fear (they certainly give the impression), honestly think they are more spiritual than others. "If you don't speak in tongues, you are not as spiritual as I am." Or, "If you haven't experienced the gifts of the Spirit, you are not really in touch with God." Such people make some Evangelical Christians feel second-class, and this attitude, which I can only call Pharisaical, helps erect a wall that divides Christians from Christians. But second, take the Calvinists. So many of them, I fear (they certainly give the impression), honestly think they are more on God's wavelength than other Christians. "If you don't believe in the sovereignty of God as we do, you are not a faithful believer." Or, "If you don't believe in predestination and the eternal security of the believer,

you don't really know the God of the Bible." Such a spirit, which I can only call pharisaical, alienates many other Christians and makes some of them feel they are theologically illiterate. As you can see, there is more than one kind of Pharisee!

25. *We call another person a Pharisee.* If I call you a Pharisee, I am a Pharisee. When I say, "The trouble with you is that you are always judging people," I just judged you. When I point the finger at you for pointing the finger, I too point the finger. "Do not judge, or you too will be judged" (Matt. 7:1). What does one do? Answer: we must learn to control the tongue. "God is in heaven and you are on earth, so let your words be few" (Eccles. 5:2). "When words are many, sin is not absent, but he who holds his tongue is wise" (Prov. 10:19).

The truth is, the Pharisee lurks in all of us. This means we would be among those Jesus condemned the most. This fact alone ought to catapult us out of our comfort zones and make us see not only our self-righteousness but also how grateful we should be that God saved us. We don't deserve to be saved. God was simply kind. Good. Merciful. He saved Saul of Tarsus, a Pharisee of the Pharisees indeed. And Saul, called Paul, never got over it. He thanked God as best he could as long as he lived.

If God could save Paul, He could save anybody. If God could save you, He could save anybody. If God could save me, He could save anybody. Why did He do it? I don't know and probably will never know. I can only spend the rest of my life doing my best to thank Him and show Him how thankful I am.

·7·

The Sovereignty of God

> "But Mr. Spurgeon, what if we convert one of the non-elect?"
>
> "Don't worry, my boy," replied the great Charles Haddon Spurgeon, "God will forgive you for that."

I did not always believe what I will teach in this chapter. I was not brought up to believe in what follows, not even remotely. The people I knew back in Kentucky who believed some of what I shall elaborate on in this chapter went to such extremes with it that it was enough to put most reasonable and thinking people right off the subject. It is hard to say which is more true: That it is the most abused teaching in church history or that, rightly understood, it is the most needed in the Church at the present time. Because I believe the latter is true, I shall do my best to introduce it, as though you knew little or nothing of it, and yet show why it is definitely needed.

My discovery of the truth of the sovereignty of God came as a result of my "Damascus Road" experience on 31 October 1955. When I refer to it in that manner, however, I do not mean my conversion, as it was in the case of Saul of Tarsus, but to a work of the Holy Spirit many years after I was saved, which I now believe was the baptism of the Holy Spirit. It led to an enormous change in my life but also my theology—not in the essentials of the faith but in very important truths of the Bible nonetheless.

It not only made the Bible become alive in my heart more powerfully than I had ever known but also led me to teachings in the Bible I did not know were there! I no longer read the Bible defensively or with the aim of proving a certain point of view. I just wanted to know what the Bible was saying and was prepared to believe it, no matter where it led.

This happened to me when I was a student at Trevecca Nazarene College (now University) in Nashville, Tennessee. I was also pastor of a small country church in Palmer, Tennessee. On the way back to Trevecca one Monday morning, the glory of the Lord filled my car and the Lord Jesus Himself was interceding for me at the right hand of God. It was as real as if it were physical or tangible. I entered into a rest of soul and experienced a peace I did not know was possible in this life. The Lord Jesus was more real to me than anything around me. If nothing more had happened, it was still the greatest experience of my life.

But more followed before the day was over. Waves of glory swept over me as I was given an infallible assurance of my salvation. I knew I was eternally saved, and with that came an awareness that what happened to me was a work of the Holy Spirit. I now know it was a sovereign work, something God *alone* did. I could not make it happen for me, and neither could I make this happen for anybody else. From this came a focus on certain Scriptures in the New Testament that meant—here comes the controversial part—election or predestination. Though such had been utterly alien to me, now this teaching was very, very real to me. I knew there was truth to it despite the fact that my old church taught against it. Some even said the teaching was of the devil and "born in hell." All I knew was it was true, despite what I had been taught as I grew up.

This drove me to the Word of God. At first I thought I was the first person to have this understanding since the apostle Paul. I thought what happened to me was unprecedented, but I was wrong. Not only was it not new, but I had tapped into the theological mainstream of the Christian Church. I was amazed to discover this and have never gotten over it. Why would God show this to me? Better still, why did God save me? What had I done to deserve to be saved? If one said, "But you followed your parents' teaching and received the Lord because you wanted to please your parents," I would say, "If that is true, why did I want to do this? Others have had Christian parents but rebelled. Why should I want to receive Jesus?"

I knew the answer was that God was being exceedingly gracious to me. I could take no credit for anything. I began to see things in the Bible for myself which made me know God was powerfully with me. What startled me most of all perhaps was that so many great men in history believed this. John Newton, author of "Amazing Grace," for example. In my church this hymn was sung almost every week. When I found out John Newton believed these things the Holy Spirit had shown me it was such an encouragement. I discovered too that the Pilgrim Fathers who settled in America believed this teaching. What thrilled me more was to discover that this teaching was central to the theology of one of my heroes—Jonathan Edwards, the leading preacher in the Great Awakening of the eighteenth century.

I have to say that it did not greatly bless my father or my grandmother. They were appalled that I had embraced a teaching they felt was contrary to the way the Lord led them. My grandmother came from the very theological background I was now upholding, but she had turned against it. Those were hard days.

I don't want to imply you are not a good Christian or that you are not following the Lord with all your heart if you do not agree with this teaching. Neither would I want to say that someone has not experienced the baptism of the Spirit if it did not lead them to the same truths I have come to embrace. As a matter of fact, I have run into countless people who have indeed received the baptism of the Spirit, and not one of them, as far as I know, was led in the same theological direction. So I am not saying for one moment that there is something wrong with you if you don't agree with me. Not at all. I simply do not understand why I have been led this way.

My mentor and professor at Trevecca, Dr. William Greathouse, who has remained a close friend over the years, said to me in astonishment in those days, "R. T., you are going off into Calvinism."

I said, "What is that?"

He replied, "We don't believe that in our church."

I retorted, "Then we are wrong." I asked him, referring to Romans 9:14–23, to explain what was meant. He said he needed more time on that—and this was some fifty years ago. "R. T., don't leave our church," he pleaded. At that stage I had no plans to leave, but it was inevitable. All who knew me in those days were absolutely convinced I would change my mind in time. My old church followed John Wesley, and though I greatly admire him, he certainly spoke against many of the things I will put forward in this chapter. He stood adamantly against the theology of George Whitefield, who espoused what I believe. Both of these men are in heaven today.

The sovereignty of God is what lay behind the betrayal of Jesus and His being crucified. It was no accident—things did not go wrong. Jesus forecast His crucifixion: "The Son of Man is going to be betrayed into the hands of men. They will kill him, and on the third day He will be raised to life" (Matt. 17:22–23). " 'My food,' said Jesus, 'is to do the will of him who sent me and to finish his work' " (John 4:34). As he further predicted His death Jesus said, " 'Now my heart is troubled, and what shall I say? Father, save me from this hour? No, it was for this very reason I came to this hour. Father, glorify your name!' " (John 12:27–28). Among Jesus' last words were these: "It is finished" (John 19:30), a translation of *tetelestai*, which was a colloquial expression in the ancient marketplace that meant "paid in full." Jesus' death on the cross was more than a crucifixion; it was atonement.

Indeed, it was what God did. "The LORD has laid on him the iniquity of us all . . . It was the LORD's will to crush him and cause him to suffer" (Isa. 53:6, 10). For this reason, when Peter preached the inaugural sermon of the Church on the day of Pentecost, he declared: "This man was handed over to you by God's set *purpose and foreknowledge;* and you, with the help of wicked men, put him to death by nailing him to the cross" (Acts 2:23). This shows that the same God who predestined the end also predestined the means to the end. This is a consistent principle in the sovereignty of God and man's role in all he does. Always. The two work together and cohere. The end in this case: the crucifixion of Jesus. It was predestined that Jesus die; He was the "Lamb that was slain from the creation of the world" (Rev. 13:8). God also predestined the means that brought this to pass—"with the help of wicked men" (Acts 2:23).

Satan prompted Judas Iscariot before his betrayal of Jesus (John 13:2). It fulfilled Old Testament prophecy (Matt. 26:15; Zech. 11:12), vindicated Jesus' own words long before the event of the betrayal (John 6:70–71), and was confirmed by Jesus' high priestly prayer when he said of the Twelve, "None has been lost except the one doomed to destruction so that Scripture would be fulfilled" (John 17:12). Nothing takes God by surprise; the same

God who predestined the end—the death of Jesus—predestined the means—those who conspired to kill Him.

This was the faith of the earliest Church. When threatened further they prayed and reminded God of their persecution and noted what Herod and Pilate did to conspire together, adding, "They did what your power and will had *decided beforehand* should happen" (Acts 4:28). This is what kept them going, God is sovereign!

Have you thought about the way Jesus introduced His parables? The way to understand the parables is to grasp the sovereignty of God. In introducing the parables He told why He spoke in parables:

> Though seeing, they do not see; though hearing, they do not hear or understand . . . Otherwise they might see with their eyes, hear with their ears, understand with their hearts and turn, and I would heal them. (Matt. 13:13, 15)

The purpose of the parables, said Jesus, is to keep those who will not be saved from being saved—or healed. Parables were to keep those for whom they *are* intended to wait until the right time for them to have them unveiled. Parables were actually designed to keep certain people in the dark. This aspect of the teachings of Jesus has been largely neglected by the Church. We all know Jesus spoke in parables, and yet we seem to sweep under the carpet His own rationale for using them—His own belief in the sovereignty of God.

To be totally candid, I don't know how people cope with any other concept of God. Who would want to pray to a God who was not in total control? And yet on both sides of the Atlantic there are church leaders who have flirted with an idea I can only call sub-Christian that maintains God does not know the future, that He waits for us to know what to do next. There is no absolute assurance that He will win out in their view. Indeed, a leading theologian from Canada who upholds this view of God was asked, "How do you know for certain that Jesus Christ will win in the end? Does not your very theology leave open the possibility that God might not win in the end?" I give him full marks for being consistent, as He agreed. And yet there were church leaders who applauded the notion.

The God of the Bible is sovereign, has a mind of His own, and knows what is going to happen because He has declared the end from the beginning. Yes, said Isaiah, "I make known the end from the beginning, from ancient times, what is still to come. I say: My purpose will stand, and I will do all that I please" (Isa. 46:10). This reminds me of a friend of mine whose six-year-old son knelt at his bedside and prayed, "God bless Daddy and Mommy and me and, oh yes, please take care of yourself because if anything happens to you we are going to be in an awful mess." If God is not sovereign, there is no hope that our Lord Jesus will triumph in the end as He did when God raised him from the dead.

I will now define what I mean by sovereignty of God: It is God's *authority* to do what He pleases with whomever He wills whenever He chooses. He does not need to explain Himself as He is answerable to nobody. The key verse for me is Exodus 33:19, which came as God's response to Moses' request to see the glory of God: "I will have mercy on whom I will have mercy, and I will have compassion on whom I will have compassion." God blesses whom He chooses, withholding judgment (which is mercy) from those who deserve it and bestowing grace (undeserved favor) on those who don't deserve it.

Here are ten passages that have utterly convinced me of the sovereignty of God. I do not list these in the order in which they came to me in my theological development, and neither are they listed with any priority of importance in mind. I begin with Matthew and work through the New Testament. To me they are all equal.

1. *"No-one knows the Son except the Father, and no one knows the Father except the Son and those to whom the Son chooses to reveal him"* (Matt. 11:27). These words of Jesus are strong. If this were the only passage like this we would be tempted to say "the buck stops with Him"; that is, Jesus. Jesus chooses who gets to know the Father. The first part of this extraordinary verse that says nobody knows the Son except the Father, and "no one knows the Father except the Son" indicates an exclusive relationship in the Godhead between the Father and the Son. Nobody gets in on it unless the Son, Jesus, selects someone who is privileged to know the Father. This verse simply means that knowing the Father and the Son occurs "by invitation only," and the Son does the inviting. There is a similar passage in Luke 10:22.

2. *"Yet to all who received him, to those who believed in his name, he gave the right to become children of God—children born not of natural descent, nor of human decision or a husband's will, but born of God"* (John 1:12–13). The one who gave the "right" was the Lord Jesus, the Word made flesh. John then makes a theological comment on why these people were enabled to receive the Lord in the first place: They were born of God. God did it. It is not the result of having parents who were regenerate (being born in a Christian home doesn't make you a Christian), it is not an act of the will (becoming a Christian is not something you can do by yourself), or of a husband's will (your spouse can't make you a Christian). It is what God does—by being born of the Spirit. You did not do anything to cause your *natu-*

ral birth; you did not choose to be born. So also with your *spiritual* birth; being born of God is done by God.

3. "*All that the Father gives me will come to me, and whoever comes to me I will never drive away*" (John 6:37). These are the words of Jesus. Whereas in Matthew 11:27 He takes the responsibility for who is privileged to know the Father, in this verse he says the Father gives His Son a people. He does not say who they are or how many they are—only that, whoever they are, they will sooner or later come to Jesus. This line of thought is echoed in His prayer in John 17:6: "I have revealed you to those whom *you* gave me out of the world . . . *you* gave them to me and they have obeyed your word." In this case He must mean the Twelve (save for Judas, see John 17:12). But He goes on to say there will be more who will believe. All those who believe do so because they were given to the Son by the Father. As to never being "driven away," this certainly means that those who come to Jesus will not be rejected. It may also mean they will be "kept" because the words literally mean they will not be "cast out."

4. "*No one can come to me unless the Father who sent me draws him, and I will raise him up at the last day*" (John 6:44).These words of Jesus indicate that no person is able to come to the Father except "by invitation." In fact, one cannot come unless the Holy Spirit drew them, and in this instance the Father takes the responsibility for the work of the Spirit. It shows man's natural state of inability to give himself life. One is born "dead" according to Ephesians 2:1,5, which means one has no natural ability to make a move unless one is given life first. This means regeneration produces faith, not the other way around. Regeneration means we have been quickened—given life. This is what enables a person to believe and why faith is God's own gift (Eph. 2:8–9).

The bottom line: It is the Holy Spirit who gives life, which leads to faith and repentance. A person is unable to respond to the gospel unless the Holy Spirit is present to grant the hearer life.

5. "*When the Gentiles heard this, they were glad and honored the word of the Lord; and all who were appointed for eternal life believed*" (Acts 13:48). It is the last part that is quite remarkable: As many as were appointed ("ordained," KJV) to eternal life believed. It would have been true had Luke said, "All who believed were appointed to eternal life." But Luke was now injecting his own theology into what had happened; you could say he was editorializing about the event of these Gentiles who were saved. Many sincere Christians may understandably wish Luke had not said that or, at least, that he would have instead said, "All who believed were ordained to eternal life." And yet that would have been a truism since it was well established that all who believe in Jesus are promised eternal life. But Luke has election and predestination in mind when he throws in this theological point of view. My Greek teacher at seminary admitted that the Greek is clear, he simply said to me, "I disagree with Luke on this." But he admitted that this statement was right here in the Bible. Agree or disagree, this is a strong affirmation of the sovereignty of God.

6. "*Paul and his companions traveled throughout the region of Phrygia and Galatia, having been kept by the Holy Spirit from preaching the word in the province of Asia. When they came to the border of Mysia, they tried to enter Bithynia, but the Spirit of Jesus would not allow them to*" (Acts 16:6–7). These verses demonstrate the sovereignty of the Holy Spirit. Jesus spoke of the sovereignty of the Spirit when He said to Nicodemus, "The wind blows wherever it pleases. You hear its sound, but you cannot tell where it comes from or where it is going. So it is with everyone born of the

Spirit" (John 3:8). It is marvelous that Paul and his friends were governed by the Holy Spirit in all they did. There are two ways of looking at these verses; either Paul and his friends were consciously being governed by the Spirit and they felt decisively led to turn from Asia or move away from Bithynia, or Luke was editorializing again and attributing their being stopped as being a sovereign, providential overruling of the Spirit. In either case it shows God's prerogative to do what He pleases with whomever He pleases whenever He pleases.

7. "*And those he predestined, he also called; those he called, he also justified; those he justified, he also glorified*" (Rom. 8:30). The Puritan William Perkins referred to this verse as the "golden chain of redemption." It is the theological biography of every believer—the stages one passes through from the time of conversion until one arrives in heaven. What makes the verse clearer is to ask: What must happen to a person before they can be glorified? Answer: That they were justified. What qualifies a person for being justified? Answer: that they were called. What must be true before a person can be called? Answer: that they were predestined.

If one has been predestined, which means the person is called "elect" or "chosen," that person will eventually be glorified. All who are predestined will be called sooner or later, which refers to the work of the Holy Spirit as in the case of John 6:44 above. And those who are called—theologians sometimes call this "effectual calling" since there is always ultimate success in the Holy Spirit's efforts to produce saving faith with the predestined, or elect—will come to faith and be justified. All those who are justified will be glorified, an implicit proof of the teaching "once saved, always saved." The bottom line: Those predestined by God, what Luke refers to as being appointed to eternal life, will eventually be called, justified, and glorified.

8. *"Just as it is written: 'Jacob I loved, but Esau I hated.' What then shall we say? Is God unjust? Not at all! For he says to Moses, 'I will have mercy on whom I have mercy, and I will have compassion on whom I have compassion.' It does not, therefore, depend on man's desire or effort, but on God's mercy"* (Rom. 9:13–16). These are probably the strongest words of all. I think it is fair to say that the word "hate" may be understood as "loved less." But the fact remains that Paul wanted to establish that Jacob and Esau—"before the twins were born or had done anything good or bad—in order that God's purpose in election might stand" (v. 11) were set in God's purpose before they were born. It rules out the notion of foreseen faith, a teaching I will refer to in the next paragraph. Paul's main point, however, is this: Being saved, justified, born again, or converted—whatever term you wish to apply—does not depend on our desire or effort; being a Christian is an incalculable privilege and is granted to us entirely because of God's mercy. God gives this mercy to whom He gives this mercy; it is His sovereign right, His prerogative. Paul is not making a case that Esau is eternally lost in hell. Martin Luther (who believed in predestination) even said he expects to see Esau in heaven. Paul just wants to show that if God can choose Jacob over Esau regarding the issue of inheritance even before either were born, He has the right to choose who receives mercy to this very day. Therefore nobody can take any credit for being a Christian; it is owing to the sheer goodness and mercy of God. Nothing more. For God is sovereign and has this right.

9. *"[God] who has saved us and called us to a holy life—not because of anything we have done but because of his own purpose and grace. This grace was given us in Christ Jesus before the beginning of time"* (2 Tim. 1:9). This verse coheres with Ephesians 1:4–5, 11 (please read) and further makes the point that God's choice of

those who become Christians was not based upon good works or foreseen faith. Some valiantly try to make the doctrine of predestination refer to what God knew in advance—that He knew who would believe and who wouldn't so He chose those He knew would believe. This is *nice* and softens the blow to a teaching that is difficult to understand. The problem is, Paul rules out this idea, both here and in Romans 9:11 (which we looked at above). Some picture God as being up high on a tall building and looking down on a parade and seeing both the end and the beginning of the parade. It is reckoned that in this way God knew who would believe and chose them in advance of their being born. This teaching is known as Arminianism, named for Jacobus Arminius (1560–1609) who opposed Calvinism, named for John Calvin (1509–1564). Since the early seventeenth century, Protestantism has been generally divided between those who are Calvinists (such as George Whitefield, Jonathan Edwards, Charles H. Spurgeon) and Arminians (such as John Wesley and virtually all the early Methodists, Pentecostals, and Charismatics). The bottom line: Paul says God's choice of us is not based on anything we do but by His grace alone, and that choice was made before time began.

10. *"They stumble because they disobey the message—which is also what they were destined for. But you are a chosen people, a royal priesthood, a holy nation. . . . Once you were not a people, but now you are the people of God; once you had not received mercy, but now you have received mercy"* (1 Pet. 2:8–10). This is a very important passage that shows the distinction between those who are chosen and those who are not; the latter are seen as disobedient. Whereas the elect are chosen without any reference to worthiness, those not saved "stumble because they disobey the message." It comes to this: If we are saved it is because of the sheer grace and mercy

of God; if we are lost it is because we are disobedient to the message of the gospel. And what about those who never hear the gospel? They will be judged by a different standard; namely, the light of creation (Rom. 1) and conscience (Rom. 2). But there is no promise such people will be saved, only that they will be judged by a different standard. But woe indeed to those who have heard the gospel and rejected it. If, however, we are justified by faith it is because we were chosen and called; if we remain in our sins it is because we loved darkness rather than light (John 3:19). Those who are lost will get what they deserve, a just judgment; those who are saved receive what they don't deserve, grace. Some get what they deserve while others get what they don't deserve. That is why it is called grace. "For it is by grace you have been saved, through faith—and this not from yourselves, it is the gift of God—not by works, so that no one can boast" (Eph. 2:8–9).

Years ago, I used to have friendly but none the less heated quarrels with my teachers and professors at seminary. They were virtually all Arminians at that time. I was seen as the resident Calvinist among the student body. I will never forget the answer given by the top Greek professor who did claim to follow the apostle Paul when I asked: "If Paul believed what I think he truly believed, how else *could* he have said it?" He replied (I admired his candor), "What he said is the only way he could have said it" had he believed what I was maintaining. So there were both professors at my old seminary who said they disagreed with what was written in the New Testament in the first place, and also those who admitted they did not want to believe what Paul said so they interpreted him according to their own bias.

What I have written in this chapter is not easy for some to accept. This is obviously because of the implication that not all are chosen. Why aren't all chosen? You tell me. I wish they were. I would have no objection if that were true, and I will be thrilled beyond words to find out one day that I got it all wrong. For if all were chosen, then all would be saved. This is known as Universalism, the belief that God is too kind to let anybody go to hell; therefore He will ensure that all will be saved in the end. I wish it were true—oh, how I wish this. But the God of the Bible does not reveal Himself in such a manner that we can make a sound doctrine out of it. I wish He were that nice.

I have made a decision I am at ease with: To love and worship the God of the Bible and to defend Him to the hilt. I love Him. "How could you?," some ask. Because I have had a glimpse of His glory and the little bit I have seen of Him is so wonderful I am prepared to say that what I don't understand about Him will be even more glorious. If you opt for the Nice God you can be comfortable with, I would lovingly caution that you could be playing into Feuerbach's hands and projecting a God on the backdrop of the universe that coheres with your own idea about Him but which is not the true God after all.

But maybe you don't want to accept the God of the Bible? That is a choice one must make. If Feuerbach's reasoning is valid, one reason I know that the God of the Bible is the true God is because Feuerbach never would have imagined that anyone would project the God I am describing in this book on the backdrop of the universe. Nobody would have come up with a God like this—He is too full of awe and, yes, terrible. "For the LORD thy God is among you, a mighty God and terrible" (Deut. 7:21 KJV; cf. Deut. 10:17; Neh. 1:5; 4:14; 9:32). The NIV never uses the word "terrible" but rather "awesome." Yes, God is awesome. But whereas the word "terrible" often means negative things we certainly would not want to say about God, the word "awesome" has come to mean what is also very complimentary, thrilling, and exciting. Feuerbach did not have a sovereign God in mind when he conceived of his rationale for being an atheist.

If the teaching in this chapter is new to you or difficult to accept, you will probably want to know how the free offer of the gospel comes into play. For example, Jesus said that "whoever believes in him shall not perish but have eternal life" (John 3:16). Paul said, "Everyone who calls on the name of the Lord will be saved" (Rom. 10:13). Indeed, "Whoever is thirsty, let him come; and whoever wishes, let him take the free gift of the water of life" (Rev. 22:17). The offer is made to all in order that those whom God has chosen will respond. The task of the evangelist is not to figure out *who* has been chosen but to try to get everybody saved; the elect alone will hear the word so as to respond in saving faith. Those who are "thirsty" and who "call" on the name of the Lord show that God has called them or they would not come to Christ in faith.

If you ask, "How do I know I have been chosen?," the follow-up question is: "Are you trusting Christ and not your good works to save you?" If the answer is yes, be assured that you have been chosen, called, and justified, and you will be glorified. The great Charles Spurgeon used to say, "Don't ask, 'Am I elected?' Ask, 'Do I believe?' "

Spurgeon fought those in his day who took an extreme view of the sovereignty of God and did little or nothing to preach the gospel to the lost—some did not even believe in the free offer of the gospel. Others were more worried about false professions being made by people not really converted than they were about the lost going to hell. When a young preacher rushed up to Spurgeon after the latter was teaching these men to plead with sinners and do all they could to win the lost, he said, "But Mr. Spurgeon, what if we save one of the non-elect?"

whereupon Spurgeon patted him on the shoulder and replied, "Don't worry, my boy. God will forgive you for that."

When we were out in the streets in London giving out tracts and doing all we could to see the lost saved, I would say to our Pilot Lights, "Speak to them as though their destiny were in your hands." I would rather regret trying too hard than being passive in the matter of soul-winning. I used to hear a sweet old man pray week after week at our prayer meetings on Sunday evenings before the service, "Lord, bring in thine elect tonight." But Spurgeon, no slave to a rigid system and in no theological straitjacket, would pray, "Lord, save all thine elect and then elect some more."

The sovereignty of God, rightly understood and applied, does not militate against zealous evangelism; it is a corrective to those who go too far in trying to make the Holy Spirit do things, as we will see below.

This teaching, rightly understood and applied, as we shall see in the following chapter, does not jeopardize evangelism; neither does it cut across one's need to know they are eternally saved. Do not let those who have abused this teaching put you off from the solid, clear, biblical teaching we are attempting to uphold in this book.

Nobody is rejected who trusts the blood of Jesus. For that blood was shed for all (2 Cor. 5:15; Heb. 2:9). Do not worry whether you are chosen, only worry whether your trust is in the blood shed on the cross. If your reliance and only hope is in Christ's blood, you are as saved and secure as the apostle Paul himself. Nobody—nobody—is turned down who puts their trust in what Jesus did for them on the cross. And yet those who do so show that God has chosen them.

· 8 ·

Why Believe in the Sovereignty of God?

> When the pure gospel is preached to people as they are it will save some and condemn others, but it will accomplish God's purpose.
>
> HENRY MAHAN

Why is this chapter important? Why should you and I believe in the sovereignty of God as I have briefly outlined so far? The main reason, apart from the obvious reason—to be in line with God's own Word—is that this teaching is a needed corrective to so many abuses that are rampant in the Church today, speaking generally. I will give the following examples.

Manipulative Evangelism

This has been done both in public appeals with high-pressure altar calls and in personal evangelism when a person is coerced to make a profession of faith without any persuasion in the heart. "A man convinced against his will is of the same opinion still," someone said. How true. Some seem to think that any profession of faith, or even baptism, proves that the person has been converted.

I happen to believe in personal evangelism. Our Pilot Light ministry at Westminster Chapel was entirely that. We talked about Jesus with total strangers in the streets between Victoria Station and Buckingham Palace. Moreover, we did all we could to lead them to Christ once the gospel was presented. We have given away tens of thousands of pamphlets in nearly thirty languages. Likely many who made professions of faith were not converted, but some were. One convert went into the Anglican ministry.

We will not know until we get to heaven how many people were led to a saving knowledge of Christ through our Pilot Light ministry, but it is personal evangelism. I did my best to be governed by the sovereignty of God in our evangelism and cautioned our Pilot Lights not to say, "Five people were saved today" but rather, "Five people prayed to receive the Lord Jesus today." Only God knows who is saved. No Pilot Light that I know of pressured people to make a decision. I taught a ten-week course on street witnessing—several of the weeks dealt with theology—and emphasized the absolute necessity of the work of the Holy Spirit in evangelism.

Evangelistic preaching that is followed by public appeals has at times done a lot of harm. The reason altar calls were not given at Westminster Chapel before I came was based on a sincere concern not to usurp the Spirit's work in persuading a person to become a Christian. When I started giving appeals at the Chapel in June 1982 I made sure there was no pressure such as singing twenty verses of "Just as I Am" or "Almost Persuaded." I even wrote a book called *Stand Up and Be Counted* which makes a case for giving appeals within the context of the sovereign work of the Holy Spirit. I have watched some evangelists and even pastors, however, play into the emotions of people to get them to walk the aisle and make a public decision for Christ.

Yet the most reprehensible thing of all is to give the impression that these people who walk the aisle, join a church, sign a card, or get baptized are actually converted. This would make God nice indeed. Nice God would not require people to be convicted of their sins by the Holy Spirit and make their calling and election sure by holy living (2 Pet. 1:10).

Only the Holy Spirit can convert a man or woman; getting people to make a public decision without the inward persuasion of the Spirit is manipulation and abuse. It is nice preachers making God look nice by promising them a home in heaven whether their hearts have been changed or not. "Just come forward, let us baptize you" (so your name can be added to the list of our many church members and make our statistics look good). This abuse of God's holy Name grieves the Spirit. The Dove flutters away and nobody feels a thing, because God is too nice to upset the vast program of the Church.

On the other hand, it seems to me that it is quite right to encourage people to respond to what they have heard—to allow them to do what they *want* to do. Peter did this after his sermon on the day of Pentecost when Luke says, "With many other words he warned them; and he pleaded with them, 'Save yourselves from this corrupt generation' " (Acts 2:40).

In J. I. Packer's classic book *Evangelism and the Sovereignty of God*, the author employs the word "antinomy"—parallel principles that seem irreconcilable but are both true. The Bible is full of these: Jesus is God and man, the Christian is simultaneous saint and sinner, God is merciful and just. Our call in evangelism is to reach all we can for as long as we can while remembering this unwavering principle: Only God saves. It is an antinomy.

When we are governed by the sovereignty of God we discover it makes all the difference in what we try to get people to do. You cannot save the non-elect and you will not dislodge God's chosen. The preaching of the gospel will save some and condemn others, but it will accomplish God's purpose. New Testament evangelism stands in stark contrast to the Nice God who would not offend anyone.

The Promise of Prosperity

One of the strongest movements in some parts of the Church at the present time is largely associated with an emphasis on what is often called the "prosperity gospel." This view suggests it is the will of God for every Christian to be prosperous, both spiritually and financially.

This message has great appeal, especially to poor people. One can appreciate how struggling families welcome a way out of their financial difficulties. When a preacher comes along and preaches prosperity—telling them it is God's will—such people will naturally say they want this. Such people are usually told they must show faith in God if they want this prosperity to come to them, and the way to demonstrate that faith is to send money to the very preacher who presents them with this good news of prosperity. The preachers never say, "Give your money to someone else, not me," but always to their very own ministry.

One can appreciate why people send in their money; they want to show God they really believe in Him. Often the preachers who appeal for people's money in this fashion are themselves very prosperous; it is shown by their clothes, the gold jewelry they sport, the posh cars they drive, not to mention their luxurious homes. Instead of putting people off, this often has the opposite effect: Desperate people think, *This must be right because this preacher seems so successful* and so they give sacrificially.

What worries me most is that such preaching plays into people's greed. Greed is something we come by naturally, not by taking a college course on how to be greedy. It is a part of the sinful flesh we inherited from our first parents after their original sin in the Garden of Eden. The apostle Paul put greed alongside sexual immorality (Eph. 5:3). When we watch television entertainers play into our sexual appetites we are not surprised; we take that for granted. But for Christian leaders to play into our greed in order to persuade us to part with our money is, in my opinion, wicked.

But is not the teaching of prosperity in the Bible? Yes, it is. It was a part of the Mosaic Law. The blessings for obedience are quite wonderful (read Deut. 28:1–14). But the promise of blessing was based not on sacrificial giving to a ministry but adherence to the whole Law of God. Prosperity, then, was promised to the godly for their obedience to the Law.

The blessing promised on the basis of financial giving was on tithing—which was to be given to the "storehouse" (Mal. 3:8-10). I have written a book called *Tithing*—reissued as *The Gift of Giving*—making the case that the New Testament equivalent to the storehouse is the local church. The tithe, which is equivalent to one tenth of your income, should be given to your own church. I go further and make the case that you cannot out-give the Lord and should give to Christian charities beyond your tithe apart from your church if you like, so long as the initial tithe was given to your church. Malachi 3:10 made a bold promise:

> "Bring the whole tithe into the storehouse, that there may be food in my house. Test me in this," says the LORD Almighty, "and see if I will not throw open the floodgates of heaven and pour out so much blessing that you will not have room enough for it."

But note: it was to be given to the storehouse.

It would appear that the overwhelming thrust of prosperity gospel teaching is from church leaders who want people to give to their ministries. If they are wanting their hearers to enjoy prosperity because this is God's will, why don't they exhort their hearers to give to their own church? Were they to do this, it would be obvious the glory of God and the building up of the saints is what such people are interested in. But that does not seem to be the case.

But the main point I want to make is this: There is no categorical promise in the New Testament that God wants you to prosper; as a result, to not prosper is thus not a result of your own lack of faith. I do believe that in the long run we cannot out-give the Lord (see 2 Cor. 9:6–9). But to say God wants you to be well off financially or to prosper materially on the condition that you will send money to this or that ministry is to cross over a line that shows contempt for the sovereignty of God. The most one should promise is that God *may* prosper you, but God is sovereign. He cannot be controlled. To use His name to gain funds for a ministry with promises of prosperity is to manipulate people and offer them hope that is beyond what God's Word guarantees. Paul said,

> I know what it is to be in need, and I know what it is to have plenty. I have learned the secret of being content in any and every situation, whether well fed or hungry, whether living in plenty or in want. (Phil. 4:12)

Preaching that godliness with contentment is great gain (1 Tim. 6:6) honors God and enables people to build up a reward in heaven. He promises prosperity in this life to some, namely those who can be trusted with great riches. But not all. The promise is, *I will have mercy on whom I will have mercy.* May the prosperity gospel ministers be gripped by God's sovereignty and their preaching renewed.

Healing

The prosperity gospel is often associated with the ministry of healing. Perhaps unfairly many refer to this as the "health and wealth" gospel. The premise is that God wants you to be rich and He wants you to be healed if you are unwell.

I doubt Paul would have gone into Corinth with fear and trembling as he did had he the authority to promise that all sick people would be healed and all poor people in financial difficulty made rich if they would accept Jesus. No need to fear with a message like that! People would flock to receive such a Jesus. No stigma, no offense. They would line up to get their healing and assurance of prosperity.

But knowing the offense of the cross as he did, Paul none the less determined "to know nothing while I was with you except Jesus Christ and him crucified" (1 Cor. 2:2). By this Paul meant that faith in Jesus means wisdom, righteousness, holiness, and redemption are put to our credit (1 Cor. 1:30). We were declared righteous before God and saved from the wrath to come—that was Paul's gospel, with not a word about healing. To find a people that would be interested in such a gospel required the anointing of the Spirit on His preaching.

Paul believed in healing. He was an instrument of the Holy Spirit and he was used to heal many times. But he did not claim the blood shed on the cross *guaranteed* that those who trust Jesus would be saved and also healed.

God has become very nice in recent times, according to some. Nice indeed. We are now told by some—often the same preachers who promise prosperity—that when Jesus died on the cross it was so we might be healed of all diseases. If we are not healed, it is because of our lack of faith.

I long to hear one of these preachers uphold the real reason Jesus died. He came to save us from our sins and to ensure that we will go to heaven, not hell, when we die. By His sacrifice we are clothed with the righteousness of Jesus and freed from the demands of the Mosaic Law. He died and rose again to bring us into intimacy with God the Father and to enable us to have communion with the Holy Spirit. This is Paul's gospel.

But it is hard to get people motivated to send in their money for this. Better results come when people are told "God wants you healed"—much more than a message like "God wants to save you from your sins." So Paul went into Corinth with fear and trembling because he knew this was not what people were interested in hearing. But he stuck to his guns and stayed with the preaching of the cross—"foolishness to those who are perishing, but to us who are being saved it is the power of God" (1 Cor. 1:18).

I watch some of these preachers who offer health and prosperity over television. They quote verses in the Bible, yes. But they often astonishingly miss the main point of the gospel and never, ever, seem to get around to preaching the real reason Jesus died on the cross. You get the impression that the reason He died was so we could enjoy living on this planet in the here and now. Existentialist teaching—what's in it for me—has found its way into the Church, largely through television, and the gospel itself has passed behind a cloud. Whatever happened to the gospel?

When Isaiah prophesied that the death of Messiah meant we would be healed by His wounds (Isa. 53:5), he promised that the Son of God would heal people. And he did. Yes, Jesus of Nazareth did just that. The miracles were so vast "even the whole world would not have room for the books that would be written" (John 21:25). Not only that, we have the promise of Isaiah that foretold this. For when the demon-possessed or physically ill were brought to Jesus and they were delivered and healed, Matthew quotes Isaiah: "He took up our infirmities and carried our diseases" (Matt. 8:17; Isa. 53:4).

But this aspect of Jesus' ministry is about the only thing some church leaders wish to focus on. They choose the part of Jesus' life and teachings that appeals to a generation interested in comfort in the here and now. It is a nice God who gives people who otherwise have little time for the true gospel what plays into their comfort zones.

J. I. Packer has referred to the Bible belt in America as being a thousand miles wide and one inch thick. That Bible belt would not be there at all had there not been at least two Great Awakenings: The first in New England in the eighteenth century and the second in the South in the early nineteenth century. Those revivals, which led to countless others all over the United States, were characterized by the preaching of the cross, the need to be ready to meet God because there is a heaven and a hell, and the changing of people's lives from promiscuous to godliness. The Bible belt today may be a shadow of what it once was, but that is partly because the preaching of today is almost a different gospel or, at the very least, a lopsided interest in the things of God for the wrong reasons.

Never forget that the apostle Paul had a "thorn in the flesh." We do not know what it was or whether it was physical or had to do with illness at all. But the fact remains that even he, God's sovereign and highly esteemed vessel, prayed three times (2 Cor. 12:8) for it to be removed! God merely replied, "My grace is sufficient for you" (2 Cor. 12:9). Paul knew God was sovereign and could give or withhold mercy, and that He would be just in acting either way. And yet believe it or not, one prominent "health and wealth" television preacher actually said, "If the apostle Paul had had my faith he wouldn't have had his thorn in the flesh." Think about that.

I believe in healing. I believe God heals today. In this book I tell the story of my wife's own miraculous healing. For I do not believe that the miraculous ended after the early Church gave us the Bible. "Jesus Christ is the same yesterday and today and forever" (Heb. 13:8). In Westminster Chapel we had regular healing services and saw genuine healings from time to time.

But God is sovereign in healing just as He is in salvation. It is not right to put sick people under a cloud of guilt because they have not been healed, which is what so many faith healers do today. I love what Randy Clark says: in the New Testament the people who were healed were not the ones required to have sufficient faith—that was for the ones who did the praying. But this is not the emphasis with most healing ministries today, I am sorry to say. They put sick people under pressure to have more faith, and such weak people blame themselves for their sickness, which is both unfair and wrong.

The main reason Jesus died on the cross was to prepare us for heaven. All who trust His blood for salvation will be saved and guaranteed a home in heaven, but not all who trust Christ's blood are healed. Salvation was the primary purpose of Jesus' death, healing was subsidiary. But the kind of preachers I am describing in this chapter make the secondary reason for the cross the main reason. Why? Because it is not the real gospel, it is counterfeit. A nice God watches all this happen and such preachers never seem to feel a thing. There is no sense of shame and no apologies for making innocent, ill people feel guilty. I knew a godly, sincere man (I was his pastor) who depleted his life savings by sending all he had to a ministry that promised it was the best way for him to be sure he would be healed. Sadly, he never was healed and soon died with nothing; he left his widow virtually penniless.

Where is the preaching of the sovereignty of God among church leaders like this? I fear it does not exist at all. Some would not believe it, for doing so would cause their ministries to disintegrate and come to shreds. For most it is built on the premise that you must show you have faith by sowing seed for the harvest of healing. So people send in their money. Nice God looks down from heaven, His heart aching, but He says nothing. For now.

I think a lot about the rise of faith healers that came when there was a really powerful anointing of healing abroad. Paul Cain told me that between 1949 and 1951 virtually everybody he prayed for was healed. Wheelchairs were stacked to the ceilings of auditoriums and tents in which he ministered. But for some reason that anointing lifted. Paul Cain himself became a recluse and decided to wait for the day when God would perhaps do it again. But others in such a ministry kept it up and would not concede that the powerful anointing wasn't around anymore. They started blaming the sick people for their lack of faith if they weren't healed and threw in the prophecy of Isaiah 53 to prove that healing was as inherent in the atonement as the promise of salvation. It was so sad and so wrong. People wanted a nice God who never says no and does not have a sovereign will.

We need a restoration of the sovereignty of God in the Church today. Let God be God. He is able to heal, but He may not choose to heal. He is sovereign. Jesus himself walked right past the lame man at the temple gate called Beautiful many times over the years and did not heal this man. It would seem Jesus saved him for Peter and John, who came along later and saw this man gloriously healed (Acts 3). The point is, Jesus Himself—who had all authority and power—walked past the man and left him unhealed. He mirrored the sovereignty of God in His ministry as does the Holy Spirit to this day. The preaching and teaching of the sovereignty of God, were it to emerge all over the Church, would encourage us to believe that:

- God is alive and real
- God has a will of His own which is to be respected
- We do not need to feel guilty when things do not happen as we would wish

The discovery of the sovereignty of God is a wonderful recipe for overcoming guilt. Perhaps God will revive the anointing of healing in great power once again. If He does, let us never forget that He who gives can also take away, and He is perfectly just either way.

Spiritual Warfare

In recent years there has been considerable interest in the subject of spiritual warfare, the demonic, and deliverance. I know some people who have devoted the whole of their ministries to this. I ran into a casual acquaintance a few years ago and asked him what he is doing these days and he replied, "I'm doing spiritual warfare these days." I wasn't sure what to say, but I know what I thought: *This man is playing with electricity with wet fingers and had better be very, very careful.* I did not know him well enough to share my thoughts. I gather he gave it up later on.

A very high-profile preacher decided he would go into a famous city in California and attack the devil. He should have known he was out of his depth. Sadly he was not surrounded with prudent people to whom he was accountable. He marched into this city and started attacking powers and authorities, believing (I assume) he could make a difference and turn that city around. Instead he was completely defeated, overcome by the enemies he proposed to attack, humiliated, and out of the ministry weeks later.

Spiritual warfare is serious, serious business. God never promotes us to the level of our incompetence. Accepting our limits is humbling but always crucial and yet perhaps never so important as in the area of the demonic.

The devil is real, the demonic is real, demon possession is real, and the attack of evil forces is ever present. Said Peter, "Be self-controlled and alert. Your enemy the devil prowls around like a roaring lion looking for someone to devour" (1 Pet. 5:8). He is always prowling around waiting for an entry point in our lives by which he can turn things upside down, bring us to despair, and make us think there is no way out.

The devil will be most happy if you will take either of these two options: first, do not believe in him at all—deny his existence entirely (he would love that); or second, become preoccupied with the demonic and the occult and go to extremes on spiritual warfare—taking the devil on, so to speak. He loves that too.

By yourself, you are no match for the devil. Don't ever take him on, don't ever pick a fight with him, and don't ever imagine yourself so strong that you can punch him in the nose and make him leave you alone. He will not only love it, but he will also divert you from the things that ought to preoccupy you and you will become virtually useless in the kingdom of God. I am sorry, but that is the way it is.

What worries me most about certain people I have come into contact with is they have a low view of the sovereignty of God and a high view of their knowledge of the devil. Some seem to concentrate on the devil more than they believe in the pre-eminent power of God. Others sadly don't seem to have much responsible fear of the devil. They deal with him as if he were a toy to play with.

There are a number of Scriptures that have governed me in this area. I pray the Holy Spirit will apply these to your life and ministry:

> Finally, be strong in the Lord and in his mighty power. Put on the full armor of God so that you can take your *stand* against the devil's schemes. For our struggle is not against flesh and blood, but against the rulers, against the authorities, against the powers of this dark world and against the spiritual forces of evil in the heavenly realms. Therefore put on the full armor of God, so that when the day of evil comes, you may be able to *stand* your ground, and after you have done everything, to *stand. Stand* firm then, with the belt of truth buckled around your waist, with the breastplate of righteousness in place. (Eph. 6:10–14)

What is often forgotten in these verses that follow is the word "stand." Four times in Ephesians 6:11–14 comes this word. Why? This discussion leads me to the first principle of spiritual warfare I put to you.

1. *Spiritual warfare is defensive.* You stand. You don't jump. You don't run. You don't even walk. You certainly don't want to slip and fall. And you don't want to go backward after you have done everything to stand. Don't try to make progress. Just stand. Because when the "day of evil" comes—and it will surely come—you make progress when you simply stand. Standing is progress when you are resisting the devil. Having told us that the devil is like a roaring lion, Peter said, "Resist him" (1 Pet. 5:9). James also said it, "Resist the devil, and he will flee from you" (Jas. 4:7). You can resist him only when he attacks. Resisting someone means they have attacked you first. You don't run

around resisting what isn't already attacking you. The very point of resistance is that it is defensive. That means being defensive as opposed to going on the offense.

2. *Don't ever attack the devil.* You wait for him to attack. If he never attacks, wonderful! Be glad. Don't lament. Consider that God is answering your prayer (if you pray it as you should), "Lead us not into temptation, but deliver us from the evil one" (Matt. 6:13). The reason spiritual warfare is defensive is because you are not promised grace if you are on the attack but only if you follow the Word of God and resist the devil when he does attack. If you do the attacking, believe me, you will have a fight on your hands too big for you. You are no match for the devil.

To quote Jesus' words, "When someone stronger [than the devil] attacks and overpowers him, he [Jesus] takes away the armor in which the man trusted and divides up the spoils" (Luke 11:22). This assumes you have been attacked first; then you have the promise of God's presence and protection.

You must wait for the devil to attack before you attack. Some people are clever but not wise. Paul showed wisdom when he did not immediately turn to the slave girl who was tantalizing the disciples. She kept saying, "These men are servants of the Most High God, who are telling you the way to be saved" (Acts 16:17). This sounds good, doesn't it? Yet the Puritan William Perkins used to say, "Don't believe the devil even when he tells the truth."

> She [this girl] kept this up for many days. Finally Paul became so troubled that he turned around and said to the spirit, "In the name of Jesus Christ I command you to come out of her!" At that moment the spirit left her. (Acts 16:18)

He waited many days. Too many don't wait; they go on the attack at once and get in over their heads.

3. *Be sure you know the Lord Jesus.* As we saw in the Introduction, some Jews who went around driving out evil spirits tried to invoke the name of the Lord Jesus over those who were demon-possessed and would say, "In the name of Jesus whom Paul preaches, I command you to come out." On one occasion,

> The evil spirit answered them, "Jesus I know, and I know about Paul, but who are you?" Then the man who had the evil spirit jumped on them and overpowered them all. He gave them such a beating that they ran out of the house naked and bleeding. (Acts 19:15–16)

This is what I mean by promoting yourself to the level of your incompetence. "As thy days, so shall thy strength be" (Deut. 33:25 KJV). Be sure you are called by the Spirit to get involved in this kind of ministry.

4. *Don't rebuke the devil directly.* You may say, "But Jesus did." I say: you aren't Jesus. I have watched sincere, good, and well-meaning people say to the devil, "I rebuke you" and keep on saying it. The devil isn't too threatened by your words. And if you aren't careful he will suddenly overwhelm you and leave you in shreds before you know what has happened. The most overlooked and neglected verse in the New Testament when it comes to spiritual warfare is in Jude 9: "Even the archangel Michael, when he was disputing with the devil about the body of Moses, *did not dare to bring a slanderous accusation* against him, but said, 'The Lord rebuke you!' " Think about that verse. Michael was presumably the highest ranking and most qualified angel in the heavenly realms to take on the devil and rebuke him and give him a piece of his mind. But no. He calmly said, "The Lord rebuke you." I would plead for those involved in spiritual warfare to ponder this verse.

God is bigger than the devil. This ought to go without saying, but I would encourage all who read these lines to know that God is superior to the devil; He is sovereign and can with a little finger wipe him out before you can count to ten. And will do this one day. In the meantime remember that the devil goes only where God gives him permission. We learn this from Job. God took the initiative and let the devil have a go at Job, but God only let him go so far (Job 1:6–12). Whenever there is a presence of evil, whether it be an attack on you or your being near a demon-possessed person, do not panic. God let it happen. He did. The devil doesn't make a move without our Heavenly Father's permission. This is perhaps the main reason the teaching of the sovereignty of God is essential to balanced and effective spiritual warfare. Don't panic when you see evil. Lean on a sovereign God who can give you victory in an instant—if you follow the rules.

The teaching of the sovereignty of God is to me most edifying and comforting. If harm has come from the abuse of this teaching, it has also come from incompetent people who take on more than they should when it comes to spiritual warfare. This part of the book could save some people a lot of heartache.

Personal Success

I need this part of the present section more than anybody I know. I will come clean with you; though I believe to my fingertips every word I have typed above, I fail again and again in putting many of these principles into practice. I am too often the world's worst in applying so many of these principles.

Here is the verse that must grip you and me: "No one from the east or the west or from the desert can exalt a man. But it is God who judges: He brings one down, he exalts another" (Ps. 75:6–7).

Of course it is true that people can come from the east and the west and exalt you or me, but not under the anointing of the ungrieved Spirit of God. Our problem is, we run ahead of God and think He is right there with us and approving all we say and do, only to discover later (sometimes years later) that what we did was in our strength and not God's, which is why we got into difficulty.

If you read *In Pursuit of His Glory* you will know I used to be a door-to-door vacuum cleaner salesman. Only yesterday Louise and I drove up to South Miami and Coral Gables and I showed her the area where I used to knock on doors and sell to the rich and the super rich. I was a pretty good salesman. I could sometimes talk a person into trading in the vacuum cleaner they bought the week before on my new one—and buy a second one for their upstairs! It was the way my dad brought me up. I started selling *Grit,* the weekly newspaper, from house to house in Ashland, Kentucky, and came to be at home knocking on strangers' doors. I have consequently been a highly driven man. Many of the marital problems Louise and I have had over the years is due to my drivenness. I was driven to prepare four sermons a week for twenty-five years in London; now I am driven to finish writing this book when I am supposed to be living in retirement. It drives Louise almost mad.

For those who are driven (whatever the cause) or have a double dose of ambition, we can be believers in the sovereignty of God in our heads but deny these very principles in our hearts. I tried very hard to bring revival to Westminster Chapel. I tried too hard. Only God can bring revival; in the same way that only God can save and convert people by the Holy Spirit.

Whereas I never raised a finger to make things happen in order to become the pastor of a church (from my church in Palmer, Tennessee, to Westminster Chapel), I tried too hard to make things happen once I became the minister.

You may be a businessperson, a physician, a secretary, a bus driver, a computer whiz, a carpenter, a teacher, or an architect. God has given you an anointing to get things done at the level of your natural competence without stress. Perhaps you are looking to make more money, to get the more prestigious position or possibly to change careers altogether. Remember these words: "Unless the LORD builds the house, its builders labor in vain" (Ps. 127:1).Unless God is behind your goals, you will not succeed.

God was angry with ancient Israel for pursuing unjust goals. "I was enraged by his sinful greed; I punished him, and hid my face in anger, yet he kept on in his willful ways" (Isa. 57:17). "Sinful greed" may be translated "unjust goals." Unjust goals are aspirations, aims, or targets we have set for ourselves but which God did not set. When we envisage a target or goal that God did not put into our hearts, we may succeed, yes, but the fallout isn't worth it. Broken health. Marriage breakup. Cold hearts. Failure as a parent. It's called "winning the battle but losing the war." Here are principles I put to you as we bring this section of the book on the sovereignty of God to a close:

1. *When it comes to the place of honor, take the lowest place.* One of my favorite parables of Jesus is when He cautioned us not go to the top table when invited to a banquet. This is because the host might have to say to you, "Take a lower place" because someone more distinguished than you may have been invited and you will be humiliated. In order to save face, then, take the least prominent seat in the room and then, just maybe, you will be invited to move to a better place and be honored in the presence of all your fellow guests. "For everyone who exalts himself will be humbled, and he who humbles himself will be exalted" (Luke 14:11). I have had to ask myself many times, do

I want to be exalted if it is not God's time—or do I want to be exalted if He does not want me to be exalted at all? My answer for both is no. What use is it to be exalted before people and have everybody notice when I know in my heart that God the Father is not behind this and is not pleased? It is only a matter of time and the truth will be out. The humiliation later won't be worth it. God wants only what is best for us and our trying to make things happen to make ourselves look good will backfire on us if we do not let Him do the exalting.

2. *Avoid the love of money.* It is called a "root of all kinds of evil" and indeed, some people, "eager for money, have wandered from the faith and pierced themselves with many griefs" (1 Tim. 6:10). Some people can be trusted with a lot of money. I have always assumed I am not one of those people. I know that a long time ago—over forty years ago, in fact—God dealt with me firmly that I was not to make a lot of money but that He would take care of me. That is the way it has been across the years. We have come to retirement after living carefully and without a lot of money over the years, and God has blessed us to exceed all expectations.

But there are those who are called to make money. Chances are, certainly if you are a Christian and walking in the Spirit, if you are called to make a lot of money it will be not because of a love for money you have but because you are motivated to accomplish extraordinary things. I have watched Christian businessmen, however, who did have a love of money—they crashed. Those the Lord loves He disciplines (Heb. 12:6). If you are governed by the love of money, you will pay dearly for it down the road. "Godliness with contentment is great gain" (1 Tim. 6:6). If God blesses you financially, fall on your face and thank Him and become a great giver to the Lord's work.

3. *Don't defend yourself when you are criticized.* Don't rob God of what He does best: the enterprise of vindicating those who are wronged. Everything God does is extremely good; you could say there is nothing He does "best" because nothing He does can be improved upon. But if I may be forgiven for putting it this way, what He does so brilliantly—it truly boggles the mind—is to clear a person's name who has been falsely accused, lied about, or hurt in any way. God is for the underdog and if you have been hurt, lied about, put down, or mistreated, you got God's attention right then and there. The problem is, we tend to want to help Him out. Big mistake. He gets off our case before you can bat an eyelash. But when we will do nothing (yes, you read it correctly) but let Him work in our behalf, we will be so glad we did. Don't necessarily expect vindication to come today or tomorrow but, if you have been the object of injustice, He took notice. Remember that the example of not giving up in praying was a widow who kept asking for justice (Luke 18:1–8). Bottom line: Don't ever ever try to clear your own name. That's God's job.

4. *Don't be overly concerned to explain yourself all the time.* My friend Pete Cantrell always says, "The greatest freedom is having nothing to prove." I think too of Shakespeare's famous words, "Methinks the lady doth protest too much." This principle obviously borders on the one above, but is not always the same thing. Sometimes there is a case of making yourself clearer if you have been unclear or misunderstood. Sometimes I don't say things as clearly as I should, even when I write. I must not be defensive but take the criticism on board and set the person free who needs to know what I meant. On the other hand, we can be too occupied with what people think and lose all sense of liberty. "Where the Spirit of the Lord is, there is freedom" (2 Cor. 3:17). When we have His smile and approval we must not trade them

in for the approval of people. If it will set the other person free, explain yourself; but if it is only to make yourself look good, opt for the liberty of the Spirit instead.

5. *Accept criticism without being defensive.* "Blessed are the meek" (Matt. 5:5). Meekness is taking criticism without being angry, retorting, or even covering up for yourself. Meekness is agreeing with the person's right to say what they say, understanding why they say it, and even turning the other cheek (Matt. 5:39). After all, they may be right! There is usually a grain of truth to all criticism we receive, even when it is unfair. The least we can do is say, "I see what you mean." Maybe it is time to say, "You are right." But never should we make the person feel bad for saying what they do. Being defensive in such a case is a dead giveaway that we are very insecure, so why give them that? Somerset Maugham said that when people ask for criticism, they really want praise. So true. When you accept criticism and compliments in much the same way, you are beginning to get free.

6. *Earnestly seek the honor that comes from God alone.* There are two verses I have sought to be governed by in this connection; the first I have already mentioned in chapter 3—John 5:44: "How can you believe if you accept praise from one another, yet make no effort to obtain the praise that comes from the only God?" In this significant verse Jesus reveals the real reason the Jews missed their Messiah—they were too enamored with the praise of people. Note that Jesus said they make no *effort* to obtain the praise (Greek, *doxa*—honor, glory, praise) that comes from God alone. We may not master the matter of not being concerned with the praise of people but we can certainly make an attempt.

The second verse is Ecclesiastes 4:4: "And I saw that all labor and all achievement spring from man's envy of his neighbor."

This verse shook me rigid one evening when I saw it clearly for the first time. It shows that what has been accomplished on our planet throughout the centuries and to the present time has been motivated by people wanting to make other people jealous; therefore they get things done to get their admiration and their sense of envy. Surely we should strive to rise above that! Do you?

If this chapter grips you, it can only be the result of the power of the Spirit at work. You must know that the majority of people hate the truths of God's sovereignty. The things contained in this chapter could not possibly mean much to someone who is hostile to the principles of God's own personal glory yet enthralled instead with the glory of man, the "What's in it for me?" and an immediate reward. Therefore if you feel the Lord tapping you on the shoulder while reading these lines, I can assure you it is because He is communicating with you, trying to get your attention, and wanting intimacy with you—as opposed to not telling the world that He is hungry (Ps. 50:12).

Let God be nice to the world by not bothering to judge, to upset people, to move them out of their comfort zones or stir them up for their lack of spiritual appetite or love for His interests. But I don't want Him to be nice to me. I would prefer, if necessary, for Him to chasten or discipline me. I want to know what is in His heart—what moves Him, honors Him, and gives Him pleasure.

He owes you and me nothing. He gives mercy to whom He will. If He shows mercy to me by letting me know He is hungry, I will in gratitude fall at His feet. I repeat: If the Lord is putting a burning in your heart, don't let Him move on as if He is finished with you; beg Him to come and stay. You will never be sorry.

Conclusion

I have not sought to make God look "good" in this book. And yet He is good. He is not nice. He is not safe. But He is good. My only hope is that you have read this book through to the end and that the Holy Spirit has stirred your heart along the way because you are indeed a seeker of truth, that you want to know the true God who is also the God of the Bible. Not the God you might be comfortable with, but the God who is there—the One than whom no greater exists.

When I was in high school in Ashland, Kentucky, over fifty years ago, my English teacher scoffed at the sermon by Jonathan Edwards "Sinners in the Hands of an Angry God" which, believe it or not, was required reading in those days. But for some reason I did not scoff. I was actually drawn to know more about a sermon that would shake New England and give America its soul.

Three years ago I had the privilege of standing on the very spot where Jonathan Edwards preached that historic sermon in

Enfield, Connecticut, in the summer of 1741. I bowed my head and prayed "O God do it again," asking that the honor of His name might be restored to a nation that has lost its soul. We will not find the true God by being selective with His various attributes, picking one (love, for example) to the exclusion of others—like His justice. The glory of God is the sum total of all His attributes. The God of the Bible is a "God of glory," as Stephen said in Acts 7:2.

We all have to decide whether we really want to find the God who is and who is there as opposed to projecting one on the backdrop of the universe, as Feuerbach put it, who will always give us that "good feeling" whenever we want it. I don't mean to be unfair, but I fear that the God who is generally portrayed in pulpits and Christian television across America these days plays directly into our comfort zone—a God who appeals only to our selfish wants rather than our truest need.

God does not want us to like Him. He wants us to know Him. God lamented of ancient Israel, "They have not known my ways" (Psalm 95:10; Heb. 3:10). We may not like His "ways"—that He works all things after the counsel of His own will (Eph. 1:11), that He suddenly and without notice hides Himself (Isa. 45:15), that His Holy Spirit can be "grieved" when we are bitter (Eph. 4:30), that He requires holy living (Heb. 12:14), that He is appeased not by our good works but only by the blood of His Son (Rom. 5:9), and that He will summon every one of us to stand before Him at the Final Judgment before consigning us to our eternal abode (2 Cor. 5:10, Rev. 20:11–15).

This book has been a brief introduction to God. It is my prayer that by now you will have come to know Him. And worship Him. You may not like Him or His "ways"—at first. Therefore I would lovingly urge you to lower your voice and humbly submit to the only God who is big enough to defeat every enemy in the universe. There is no God like Him. All others are idols we have created in our minds to give us that "good feeling."

I close with the greatest paradox imaginable: the very God described in this book is One whom, were you to get to know Him indeed, is so wonderful that you would not change a single thing about Him even if you could. Because He is good. Not nice. Not safe. But good.

May the blessing of God Almighty—Father, Son, and Holy Spirit—be upon you today and evermore. Amen.

Bibliography

Kendall, R. T. *The Anointing: Yesterday, Today, Tomorrow.* Nashville: Nelson Books, 1999.

Kendall, R. T. *Are You Stone Deaf to the Spirit?* London: Evangelical Press, 2000.

Kendall, R. T. *Sensitivity of the Spirit.* Florida: Strang Communications, 2002.

Kendall, R. T. *The Parables of Jesus.* London: Sovereign World, 2003.

Kendall, R. T. *Understanding Theology.* London: Christian Focus, 1996.

Lewis, C. S. *The Lion, the Witch and the Wardrobe.* New York: HarperCollins, 2005.

Merriam-Webster's Collegiate Dictionary, 11th Edition. Springfield: Merriam-Webster, 2003.

About the Author

Dr. R. T. Kendall was born in Ashland, Kentucky, in 1935. He attended the undergraduate program at Trevecca Nazarene University in Nashville, Tennessee, receiving an A.B. degree. In 1972, he received his Master of Divinity degree from Southern Baptist Theological Seminary in Louisville, Kentucky, and an M.A. from the University of Louisville in 1973. He completed his Doctorate in Philosophy at Oxford University in England in 1977 and went on to serve as the Senior Minister of Westminster Chapel in London for twenty-five years. He has authored over forty books. He now lives in Florida with his wife, Louise. From there, he continues his career as a popular Christian preacher and writer. His best-selling books include *The Thorn in the Flesh*, *Tales of Total Forgiveness*, and *The Anointing: Yesterday, Today, Tomorrow.*

Also by R. T. Kendall

The Anointing: Yesterday, Today, Tomorrow

The Day the World Changed

The Gift of Giving

Great Christian Prayers
(compiled and edited with Louise Kendall)

In Pursuit of His Glory

Pure Joy

Sensitivity of the Spirit

Tales of Total Forgiveness (with Julia Fisher)

Thanking God

The Thorn in the Flesh

Total Forgiveness

Worshipping God